GRAPEVINE

Dave Balter is the founder and CEO of BzzAgent, Inc., the advertising industry's best known word-of-mouth marketing and media channel. Since its launch in 2002, BzzAgent has amassed a network of 400,000 consumer volunteers who have participated in nearly four hundred word-of-mouth campaigns.

Balter has been featured everywhere from the *CBS Evening News* to the BBC to *The New York Times Magazine*. He cofounded the Word of Mouth Marketing Association (WOMMA) and currently serves as a board member and chair of the association's international committee. The AdClub named him a "Future Legend" in 2008, and the year prior he was dubbed one of Boston's "Hottest Technology CEOs" by Harvard Business School. Balter was named to the "40 Under 40" list by the *Boston Business Journal* and Advertising Specialty Institute. *Women's Wear Daily* named him one of the "Top 7 Individuals Changing the Face of Beauty."

Balter's second book, *The Word of Mouth Manual, Volume II,* has just been published.

Grapevine

Why Buzz Was a Fad

but *of* Mouth

Is Forever

———

Dave Balter

PORTFOLIO

PORTFOLIO

Published by the Penguin Group

Penguin Group (USA) Inc., 375 Hudson Street, New York, New York 10014, U.S.A.
Penguin Group (Canada), 90 Eglinton Avenue East, Suite 700, Toronto, Ontario,
Canada M4P 2Y3 (a division of Pearson Penguin Canada Inc.)
Penguin Books Ltd, 80 Strand, London WC2R 0RL, England
Penguin Ireland, 25 St Stephen's Green, Dublin 2, Ireland (a division of Penguin Books Ltd)
Penguin Group (Australia), 250 Camberwell Road, Camberwell, Victoria 3124, Australia
(a division of Pearson Australia Group Pty Ltd)
Penguin Books India Pvt Ltd, 11 Community Centre, Panchsheel Park,
New Delhi – 110 017, India
Penguin Group (NZ), 67 Apollo Drive, Rosedale, North Shore 0632, New Zealand (a division of
Pearson New Zealand Ltd)
Penguin Books (South Africa) (Pty) Ltd, 24 Sturdee Avenue, Rosebank, Johannesburg 2196,
South Africa

Penguin Books Ltd, Registered Offices:
80 Strand, London WC2R 0RL, England

First published in the United States of America by Portfolio, a member of Penguin Group
(USA) Inc. 2007
This paperback edition with a new preface published 2008

10 9 8 7 6 5 4 3 2 1

PUBLISHER'S NOTE

This publication is designed to provide accurate and authoritative information in regard to the
subject matter covered. It is sold with the understanding that the publisher is not engaged in
rendering legal, accounting or other professional services. If you require legal advice or other
expert assistance, you should seek the services of a competent professional.

THE LIBRARY OF CONGRESS HAS CATALOGED THE HARDCOVER EDITION AS FOLLOWS:
Balter, Dave.
    Grapevine : the new art of word-of-mouth marketing / Dave Balter and John Butman.
        p. cm.
    Includes index.
    ISBN 1-59184-110-0 (hc.)
    ISBN 978-1-59184-228-6 (pbk.)
        1. Word-of-mouth advertising.   2. Viral marketing.   I. Butman, John.   II. Title.
    HF5827.95.B35   2005
    659.13'—dc22   2005048942

Printed in the United States of America
Set in Granjon—Designed by Joe Rutt

To everyday people
and their opinions

Contents

Preface

Normally, the preface to a book like this would be written by someone famous. If the publishers couldn't dredge up any real famous people, they'd settle for a somewhat recognizable name or at the very least an "expert in the field." It's a kind of celebrity endorsement, the book equivalent of Tiger Woods wearing the swoosh. It's the publisher saying, "Hey everyone, this famous person cared enough to write something or other for this book, so it must be good! Please read?"

The idea is that if you don't recognize the author or like the cover, then maybe the words "Preface by SOMEONE WHOSE NAME YOU KNOW" will entice you to pick up the book and find out what they have to say. Hopefully it will be compelling enough that you carry the book to the checkout counter.

Obviously, I'm not famous, nor is anyone else who might have written this preface (this is a CONTEST-WINNING preface, you see*). I don't run a successful multimillion-dollar business, I haven't done anything especially remarkable on the world stage, and so far I've avoided being the subject of a YouTube meme. I'm

---

*Hundreds of BzzAgents submitted potential prefaces for this book!

really not anyone special—and yet the very important job of convincing you to buy this book seems to have fallen to me.

Why on earth would Dave Balter entrust me with this task? We've never even met and yet in some small way, the fate of his product—this book—rests in my hands. Why would he do this? Because the whole point of the book is that the fate of all products, the fate of *your* products, rests in my hands.

I mean, not mine alone. I'm no one special. But people like me, people who try out new things and then complain or rave about them to their friends, play a huge role in the success and failure of the many, many products that are created and marketed each year. We chat with people at parties, we email our friends, and we change our Facebook status to things like "is in love with his new bread maker." Then our friends tell their friends and the message spreads.

If you're a marketing person reading this, I've gotta say I don't envy you. You guys have it rough these days. We really don't trust you and we do our best to resist you. You interrupt us all the time. You keep making us sit through five minutes of ads *before* the trailers (which are also ads) before the movie starts. You've plastered our roads with billboards, you've filled our inboxes with spam and our browsers with pop-ups. And lately, you've started making me watch short films while I try to pee at a bar. You go to all these lengths to get my attention and for what? The sad truth is that even when you do break through and get me to notice and then remember your message, I DON'T TRUST YOU.

I *do* trust my friends though. I go to the restaurants that they tell me are good. I try out the painkillers that have worked for them. I go to the concerts that they think I'll like. When it comes to big-ticket purchases, step number one is always, "Ask around."

Think about how crazy this is: marketing teams are spending lots and lots of cash on a losing battle to try to get my attention while my friends are selling me products for free. FOR FREE! What if instead of wasting all that time and effort on being ad eighty-seven of a total of two thousand in the newspaper, you could get your product into my friends' hands? Give them a chance to check it out, decide what they think about it, and then pass on the good news to the rest of us. That seems nice, doesn't it? I'd get less noise in my life and more news I can use, and you'd get a sales force hundreds of thousands of people strong who are all working for no commission and who are all individually tailoring your sales pitch for a specific prospect.

In the end, it probably doesn't matter *who* wrote the preface to this book because you probably aren't buying the book based on the preface (I'm not famous, so why would you?) because of banners or stacks of books on the front table that bombarded you at the entrance to the bookstore. You are probably buying it because a friend or colleague mentioned it to you. They said it had some cool ideas and you thought, "Hey, maybe I'll check that out." Word of mouth can be more effective than traditional marketing and it can work much better than a celebrity endorsement. Thus, in the grand scheme of things, there was really no one better to write this preface than me: an average, everyday guy who happens to know what he likes and is willing to share it.

Tim Maly (BzzAgent lot49a)
January 28, 2008
Toronto, Ontario, Canada

1

Introduction: Welcome to the Grapevine

Like every other marketer in the world, I thought I knew what word-of-mouth was all about.

Word-of-mouth? Sure. That's the uncontrollable thing that happens after a brilliant marketing campaign. Those humble little consumers glom onto the marketing messages and, pretty soon, BOOM! word starts spreading like wildfire. It's like taking aim at a target and throwing a dart at it. When you hit the bullseye, a million other darts somehow get triggered and they're all flying through the air—and thumping into other targets, which let loose a million more darts. Darts are flying, people are talking. Your product's on everybody's lips, and it takes hardly any effort on your part. Sweet!

That's what I thought. That's what I'd been told for as long as I could remember. Yes, there were those few instances when a product would generate spontaneous word-of-mouth without a brilliant marketing campaign to get the darts flying. But those, everybody thought, were anomalies and accidents, or the result of just the right customer finding out about just the right product at just the right time.

Then one day in early 2001, I was sitting in a meeting at an ad agency. I ran a promotional marketing firm at the time, and I was there as a member of the launch team for a new car model. We were about to view the rough cut of a thirty-second TV spot that would be the crown jewel of this big, fat, expensive, national marketing campaign. Before rolling the commercial, the advertising account exec leaned over to the car company client and said, with a wink, "This spot is gonna be viral. It's gonna create buzz. It'll be better than word-of-mouth."

At the time, there was a lot of chatter about the "end of marketing as we know it" and the "death of the thirty-second spot," and all kinds of new and "alternative" methods of marketing were popping up. Everybody was yammering about viral marketing, buzz campaigns, seeding, shill marketing, guerrilla marketing, and street teaming. And word-of-mouth.

But it was totally obvious that the client, as well as most of us in the room, had no idea what the ad agency exec was saying. We didn't really know what *viral* meant or what buzz really was. We didn't have a clue about their connection to word-of-mouth. But, DAMN, everybody really liked the sound of those words. They knew they were just what the product needed if it was ever going to reach its audience.

"Sounds GOOD!" the client said. "Let's roll it!"

The spot came on with all its hipness and coolness and hotness and in-ness. After it ended thirty seconds later, everybody clapped and smiled and gushed. The client bought the spot. The car company launched its big, fat marketing campaign. And when the commercial aired, not a single customer bothered to tell anyone else about it. It buzzed itself into oblivion.

That's when I began to realize that I wasn't much different

from the car company client. I was essentially clueless. I too was blathering about buzz and viral and shill and word-of-mouth and lumping them all together into one big pot of stuff that I pretty much defined as "nontraditional marketing."

There was nothing particularly wrong with that TV spot. It didn't fail because TV advertising had completely lost its mojo. It didn't bomb because everybody was blocking it with their dreaded TiVos or watching HBO or playing video games. In fact, it didn't really fail at all. It created awareness for the car. Many more people knew that this new car existed after seeing the spot and the print ads and the Web banners and the billboards than had known before. How could they not?

But they didn't talk about it. There was absolutely nothing to say. People were talking about plenty of other products, however. Why hadn't this ad generated word-of-mouth?

That's when it occurred to me that the conventional wisdom about word-of-mouth was fundamentally wrong. Generally, people thought of word-of-mouth as the byproduct of a brilliant marketing campaign or as a reaction to some unexpected occurrence. The marketer generally thought of word-of-mouth as coming about in a sequence: (A) Conduct brilliant marketing campaign. (B) Word-of-mouth will follow. But the experience of the car campaign, the TV spot, and all the stuff I had been listening to and thinking about made me realize that the traditional image was all wrong. It wasn't that the marketing dog was wagging the tail of word-of-mouth. No, the great big bushy tail of word-of-mouth was actually wagging the miniature poodle of marketing.

I thought to myself, word-of-mouth is this amazingly powerful force that everybody knows about but nobody really understands. It's rarely caused by marketing. It's not driven by marketing. Word-of-mouth is a fundamental human activity of immense depth and power. Marketing can only tap into it. Maybe.

That's when I decided to become a word-of-mouth pilgrim. To set off on a journey of discovery. Just as some people set out in search of truth, adventure, or the perfectly frothy head on a glass of beer, I decided to try to understand the most powerful marketing force in the world: word-of-mouth.

I sold my marketing services agency. I took a little office in a shared space in downtown Boston. I spent my days reading everything I could get my hands on about word-of-mouth and social networks and storytelling and consumer engagement and marketing measurement and string theory, and, when I couldn't read anymore, I played backgammon.

One day I was contemplating lunch when one of my office mates, Eric Puterbaugh, came flapping into my office, interrupted my ponderings of roast beef, and started yammering on about a book he had been reading, *Butterfly Economics* by Paul Omerod, a British economist. "He writes about how economic theory has changed in the past few decades," Eric said, as if he had just had a revelation. "His key point is that the impact of an economic event can be determined by the power of individuals." My first reaction was to wonder if Eric might have an extra bag of chips handy. Roast beef without chips seemed somehow flawed. But, instead, I said, "This is news? Of course, people have an impact on events."

Eric persisted. "Omerod is saying that all the standard theories about how economics work are wrong. They don't take into account how people perceive an economic event, which is ultimately what determines the outcome. No longer can you lower interest rates and know exactly what will happen to development of new housing, for example. You have to take into account what people think about the change in interest rates. How they com-

municate with each other about it. You have to watch their behavior, listen to their dialogue, and then—and only then—will
the outcome become evident."

Was this as interesting as Eric seemed to think? Possibly. But
not as interesting as roast beef and chips. I thanked Eric and he
moved on.

That night I was watching TV, flipping through the channels,
and thinking about what Eric had said. Who actually watches
commercials? I wondered. How do they communicate about
what they've seen to others? Could Omerod's ideas about economics also apply to TV ads? Maybe it's how people communicate with each other about the ads that determines the results of
the messages in the ads, more than the ads themselves?

Then a simple but provocative idea hit me. It wasn't *what* Eric
had said to me that was so interesting. It was that he had said it to
me at all. What made Eric decide he had to interrupt my lunch
musings to tell me about this particular book? What was it that
made him want to go out of his way to share his opinion with me,
to take time out of his day to share an experience? What was it
about our social fabric that allowed, or even demanded, that this
dialogue take place?

I hopped into the shower. I do my best thinking there. As I
shampooed, it struck me there must be a connection between the
marketing messages people receive, their individual reactions to
them, the interactions they have about them with other people,
and how they act on those messages.

I grabbed the loofah, wondering if there might be some way to
tap into that dialogue. What if a company could be created that
would help accelerate and augment those interactions and exchanges? A company that would somehow connect the little
marketing dog with its great big word-of-mouth tail?

I spent the next few months working on the idea and trying it out on investors, friends, and just about anybody else who would listen. I would rave on about *The Tipping Point* and *Anatomy of Buzz* and Pattie Maes's studies of word-of-mouth algorithms and ant theory. "What if we could tap into the power of people's opinions?" I said over and over. "What if we could help companies somehow become a part of the everyday conversation about their products?" That was the drumbeat. "What if we could create a company that would be the real-people part of the marketing process?"

Most people I spoke with didn't get what I was talking about. People with marketing backgrounds, in particular, couldn't get past their idea of the consumer as the target of the marketing process, not as a part of it. "Companies don't want to buy word-of-mouth opinions," one potential investor told me. "What they care about is the number of impressions. You'll never be able to reach enough people through word-of-mouth networks to make a difference in sales." (Needless to say, he didn't pony up any cash.)

Fortunately, their objections did not deter me.

Today, BzzAgent, the company I founded, is the world's leading word-of-mouth services provider. We have more than four hundred thousand real, every-day people in our volunteer community, and manage many other volunteer word-of-mouth communities for some of the biggest brands in the world.

Consumers join communities like ours because they are fascinated by products and services and the companies that create them. They want to get involved with them. They want to talk about them and engage in dialogue with others about them. With their involvement, we have created campaigns for clients, large and small, for-profit and not-for-profit, in all kinds of endeavors.

Within three years, we have grown from nothing to a major new force in marketing. We've made some money. We've attracted lots of attention. We've been the subject of a cover story in the *New York Times Magazine*.

Most important, I learned much more than I bargained for on this journey of discovery. About what word-of-mouth is, why we engage in it, how it proliferates, and what it can and can't do for products and services. That's why I decided to write this book— to share the knowledge. I didn't want it to be *The BzzAgent Story,* but I did want to write from the point of view of a word-of-mouth practitioner rather than that of the theoretician. I've spent three years deep inside this sometimes crazy word-of-mouth community. I've read thousands of reports from our volunteers— everybody from paroled felons to practicing nuns—about how and why they engage in word-of-mouth. I've talked with hundreds of clients about how they think about and use and measure word-of-mouth. And I've become obsessed with observing the workings of word-of-mouth in everyday situations, from baby classes to overseas business flights. So, although BzzAgent serves as the model for the book and the source of a great deal of what I know, the book goes way beyond the story of the company.

Here's the CliffsNotes version for you. (If you want, you can read the next two pages, put the book down, and tell everybody what it's about. Most of us do that with books anyway. But, of course, you won't really know what the book is about if you do that.)

- *Everybody talks about products and services,* and they talk about them all the time. Word-of-mouth is NOT about identifying a small subgroup of highly influential or well-connected people to talk up a product or service. It's not about mavens or bees or celebrities or people with specialist knowledge. It's about everybody.

- *Word-of-mouth is fundamentally different from other "alternative" forms of marketing.* Word-of-mouth marketing is not the same as buzz marketing or viral marketing and it has nothing to do with shill marketing—which involves people being paid to recommend a product without disclosing their relationship with the marketer. (Ugh.) Word-of-mouth is the honest, genuine sharing of real opinions and information about products and services. It can be stimulated and accelerated, but it can't be controlled. Marketing mediums are not the same as real word-of-mouth.

- *Word-of-mouth proliferates in unpredictable ways.* It ripples out in generations. It crosses from network to network. It takes many paths. It does not proliferate within demographically defined communities. It does not move in a predictable sequence.

- *There are limited word-of-mouth windows.* People will generate word-of-mouth only for certain periods of time, usually when the product is new or has gone through some change or when something noteworthy or ridiculous has happened to make it worthy of talk. (Paris Hilton's T-Mobile Sidekick gets hacked into. President Bush is seen riding a Trek bike.) Individuals also have limited word-of-mouth windows, during which they are interested in generating and exchanging word-of-mouth on a particular topic. If you miss the window, nobody talks.

- *Word-of-mouth is product storytelling.* It is not about people passing along marketing messages. People tell stories about products. The stories are made up from their own experiences and those of others. The marketing messages get woven into the word-of-mouth stories, but they get changed in the process. Everything about the product—the marketing of the product, and the company that offers it—is storytelling material.

- *Word-of-mouth does not have to be positive to be good.* This is not the same as "All PR is good PR." Products are never perfect and people accept that. Negative word-of-mouth can be weirdly powerful. It can add credibility to a product. If the company responds positively to negative word-of-mouth, it can turn detractors into loyalists. Negative word-of-mouth can often bring out the quiet advocates—who can be even more powerful than everyday fans.

• *Word-of-mouth is the basis for a new approach to marketing.* WITH marketing is about companies allowing everyday people into their process, giving them more interaction with the product, recognizing them more, and listening to them better. (As opposed to the traditional AT marketing, which treats consumers like targets and messages like darts.) Word-of-mouth is a source of tremendous product knowledge and marketing power. It's time to close the gap between word-of-mouth and marketing-speak and get a dialogue going between the two.

I would never have been able to come to my current understanding of word-of-mouth (as incomplete and imperfect as it still is) without the members of the BzzAgent community. So, when it came to writing the book, it was obvious and natural that they would be involved with it. Not only do their stories figure heavily in the text (and in the special chapter at the end), they have offered their help and opinions about the ideas in the book, its structure, its title, and even the cover design. This is their book as much as it is mine.

When I thought about how to translate our collective knowledge into a manuscript, however, I knew I faced a little problem: I don't know how to write a book. I can write, but that's not the same as writing a book. Besides, I had a business to run. So I found John Butman, one of the geniuses behind *Trading Up: The*

New American Luxury. In addition to book writing, he spent many years in the world of marketing communications, working with clients all over the world to develop messages, create media, and run campaigns. So he is more than just a writer, he is a thought partner and collaborator, which is why his name is on the cover with mine. (But below mine, because I'm an egomaniac.)

There was one other problem to overcome. As I said, I wanted this book to be more than just the musings of an armchair theorist. I wanted the reader to see the whole evolution of a word-of-mouth campaign, from consumers' first moment of awareness, to their word-of-mouth interactions and storytelling, to their decision to buy (or not), to their transformation into loyalists.

Seeing the whole arc of the process is critical to understanding the philosophy of word-of-mouth and to recognizing how we've captured the most honest form of marketing and learned more than we ever bargained for.

But no story of a single real campaign or any single agent would do the trick. So, we created a fictional narrative (although based on real campaigns) that features a character named Bardo (loosely based on a real BzzAgent), a fictional product called SparklyPerfect (please, do not look for it in stores), and a made-up marketer named Andie. (Hello, clients! She is not you unless you want her to be.) The narrative is contained in minichapters that alternate with the main ones. It allows us to get inside the heads of the consumer and the marketer and to understand what each one goes through during the course of an entire campaign.

The bulk of the book, however, is composed of stories of real consumers, real marketers, real products, and real campaigns.

This is, simply, the story of word-of-mouth.

The grapevine of marketing that connects us all.

Bardo, Your Average Unique Consumer

Bardo is your average American consumer.

He is a man of well-defined demographics. Male. 34. Middle manager of the dairy department for a grocery chain store. Lives in a desirable second-tier city with his wife, Megan, 33, a freelance graphic designer. Daughter Lily, age 7, attends 2nd grade. They own a home with 4 bdrms, hot tub, large yard with gas grill and outdoor oven. Household income $76,000. They own a pet skink (a trendy reptile) named Fifi.

Is this man an influential? A maven? A transmitter? Doesn't matter.

One thing is certain: Bardo lives and breathes products and services, and talks about them every day. In fact, this midmarket, middle-income, dairy department middle manager thinks of himself as a bit of a trendsetter. The Cayce Pollard (see *Pattern Recognition* by William Gibson) of the supermarket set. No, he's not into metrosexual fashion, flavored vodkas, or self-help books. But he is very big on beer, camping gear, household gadgets, freezer mitts, and social trend books.

One day, things get a little crazy in the dairy department, what with a Mexican cheese promotion and trouble with a leak in the low-frost freezer units, and Bardo is late leaving work. He stashes his new HotFinger™ freezer mitts—the ones with the double-welded fingertips, chainmail wrist guards, waterproof shell, and felted purple lining—and dashes to his two-year-old sport truck with the cold-weather package, on which he'd gotten a fantastic, end-of-season deal.

Dinner is over, but Megan has saved a plate of pasta for him. Bardo pops it in the microwave (the one with the autobrowning feature) and snaps open the fridge to grab a beer. He is delighted to discover the six-pack of the new handcrafted amber ale he had picked up the day before. A guy at work had recommended it to him, and the shelftalker at the liquor store had pushed him over the edge to try it. Bardo studies the label, thoughtfully pours the beer into the glass. Examines the color. Takes a swig. Primo.

With pasta and beer at hand, Bardo clicks on the TV (he hasn't gone flat-screen yet, but is working up to it) and surfs the channels. A spot for the amber ale catches his eye. It features an animated moose who, for some reason, lives in an igloo. The beer, which Bardo is just sipping, suddenly tastes a bit like fur.

Megan calls to Bardo that it is time to say goodnight to Lily.

"How was school?" Bardo asks his daughter, as he sits beside her.

"Dad, can we get a SparklyPerfect?"

Bardo flinches. SparklyPerfect? What could that be? Could it be the new Barney? Will he soon be spending a fortune on the SparklyPerfect equivalent of purple di-nosaur merchandise?

"Why do you want a SparklyPerfect?" Bardo asks, as he tucks her in.

"You know that girl Kendra at school?" Lily murmurs.

"Yes."

"Her dad got one."

"But you hate Kendra, don't you?"

"Yeah. But she's smart and she has good taste in this kind of thing."

"What kind of thing?"

Lily has fallen asleep.

Later, Bardo Googles SparklyPerfect, and finds his way to sparklyperfect.com.

"SparklyPerfect," he reads. "The new household wonder that adds culinary sparkle to the kitchen and is perfect for the patio and garden, too! Beyond Awesome!" Lily and Kendra were talking about kitchen gadgets?! You never know.

Although the site is a little long on cool and a little short on info, the product looks interesting. Bardo and Megan are planning their annual spring neighborhood barbecue and SparklyPerfect might be just the thing. Every year he likes to have some new gadget to show off to his friends.

Bardo bounces around the Web, but can't find much about SparklyPerfect on the techie or consumer goods blogs. There are a couple of goofy articles, obviously PR placements, from regional newspapers about how SparklyPerfect will change your lifestyle and sense of self-worth.

"Hey, Megan!" Bardo calls to his wife, who is in the bath with a glass of her favorite new wine, a California vermentino. "Have you heard anything about this Sparkly-Perfect thing?"

"I hear it's expensive!" she replies, above the sound of the bathwater starting to glug down the drain.

"Hmm." But Bardo decides to enter his email address to get more information and receive a special promotional offer.

As he falls asleep that night, Bardo goes over the arrangements for the coming barbecue. Slow-roast chicken sausage. Tasting of seasonal lagers and ales. Tricks by Fifi the skink. (She can balance a potato chip on her nose and flip it into her mouth.)

And maybe a new gadget to show off: SparklyPerfect.

2

Who Talks about Products and Why?

Everybody talks about products, all the time.

I mean everybody. That's the key to the word-of-mouth phenomenon. Everybody talks to everybody else about products every day. From the anticonsumerist PhD to the teen in baggy sweatpants, flipped hat, and ultrajammin' ride, everybody speaks the language of products and services.

When we started BzzAgent, however, we didn't understand this. We thought that word-of-mouth was created by in-the-know, early-adopting, technically focused, 18-to-24-year-old, coastal hipsters. That's what all the word-of-mouth experts said. Our plan was to build a network of these supercool or superconnected people and get them involved in creating word-of-mouth campaigns for paradigm-smashing clients who had bleeding-edge new products and services to introduce to the world.

So, we created this thing called BzzAgent and invited people to join, expecting that we would soon be electronically high-fiving with the hippest dudes and dudettes on the planet. That's not how it happened.

We were lucky enough to make the decision that we should let absolutely anyone be a BzzAgent. In our desire to build a network as fast as possible, we figured we shouldn't prohibit anyone from signing up. Besides, it would've cost money and time to build a filtering system. So, all kinds of people signed up to be BzzAgents. They weren't all young—50 percent of them were over twenty-five, 35 percent were over thirty-five. Plenty of them were downright elderly. And I don't mean fifty. I mean eighty-plus. They weren't all coastal. They lived in places all over the United States and Canada. They weren't predominantly guys, as we first expected. Seventy percent of them were women.

Most important, they were not all graphic designers or techno-geeks or marketing mavens or Web junkies or glad-handers and networkers. They were housewives and students, senior-level ex-ecutives, teachers, and dairy department managers. We really do have a paroled felon. Teenage stoners. People with large butts. Religious zealots.

What connects them? Why do they take part in the BzzAgent community? "I do it mostly for fun," BzzAgent Kyrie, a univer-sity administrator, wrote, "but also because it makes me feel like I am sharing something I believe in with the people with whom I associate." BzzAgent Angboy, a hospital psychologist, wrote, "I do it mainly to see and try out new products, and to have some impact on the products, whether through sharing with those around me or providing my own feedback to companies."

What does a BzzAgent actually do? A client, like Kellogg's or Energizer or Ralph Lauren or Anheuser-Busch, partners with us to create a word-of-mouth campaign for a specific product or service. To overly simplify the process, we ask for volunteers from the BzzAgent community to participate in the campaign, and create slots for a certain number of them, based on the crite-ria we've established with the client. The agents are provided with materials that help them understand and experience the product (usually including a free sample or coupons to purchase samples at a store) and then they talk about, or "Bzz," the product when and where they see fit. They don't hide the fact they are BzzAgents. In fact, they often talk about being a BzzAgent as much as they talk about the product itself. Whenever they have a word-of-mouth interaction about the product, they send us a report. We analyze the reports and share our results with the client.

For a client, the ultimate goal of a word-of-mouth campaign may be to increase sales of its product or to change perceptions or raise awareness. Whatever else it is about, a word-of-mouth campaign is always intended to generate credibility. But we quickly realized that there is value in what can be learned from the reports about how products are being viewed and used by all kinds of people in all kinds of situations. It is information that is far richer and more real than focus group findings, survey data, or even shop-alongs and in-home interviews.

What's more, the thousands and thousands of reports we have gathered provide an amazing window onto the behaviors and attitudes people have toward word-of-mouth and products in general. They have given us a remarkable understanding, with incredible proof, of just how much of our everyday conversation is about products and services. We really do talk about products and services all the time. "Unless you have managed to separate yourself from people completely," BzzAgent SkeletonKey wrote, "you probably Bzz several times a day without even realizing it."

Try it for yourself. Take a day and listen carefully to your conversations and interactions. Take note of how many times you talk about products in your word-of-mouth interactions. The mentions don't have to be brand names. Just products in general. You'll be amazed at how many references there are to foods, books, electronics, cars, spas, airlines, medicines, shampoos, clothes, restaurants, furniture, and God knows what else.

When I first started working with Butman on this book, he

said that he didn't think he talked about products that much. Early on, he sent me an email saying, "I was at a baseball game today, then went to a wedding. Nobody talked about products at either event. Hmm."

I wrote back, "What?" I wondered if John lived in some sort of social bubble. "Seriously," I wrote, "I can't believe no one talked about any products or services . . . but I've been wrong before."

A little later he replied, "Actually, I'm totally wrong. At the baseball game, we talked about folding canvas chairs with built-in cupholders (it was my son's game, where you bring your own chair to sit on the sideline), baseball uniforms, bottled water, cars (I showed some friends how my hardtop convertible roof folds down), and restaurant food. At the wedding, we talked about adventure vacations, cameras, wine, tuxedos, shoes, movies, books, real estate, boats, and other stuff I've probably forgotten."

In 2005, we developed a joint word-of-mouth study with Walter J. Carl, a PhD and assistant professor in the Department of Communication Studies at Northeastern University. We surveyed a sample of BzzAgents and of "everyday people." The results showed that, for both groups, it is very common for people to have interactions that include one or more product references. Everyday people (those not associated with BzzAgent) reference a product, brand, or service in about 14 percent of their interactions each week. BzzAgents are an even more product-oriented bunch—over 25 percent of their weekly interactions make reference to products, brands, and services. In the study, we also learned there are no major differences in the amount of word-of-mouth engaged in by people according to sex, age, income, or other demographic variables.

And what's comfortingly old-fashioned about these word-of-mouth interactions is that the vast majority of them take place face-to-face. Even with about forty million blog readers in the United States and trillions of emails sent a year (one estimate is that more than one hundred billion are sent each day), 80 percent of word-of-mouth occurs off-line. That's right, 80 percent of word-of-mouth is real time; real people talking to each other in the real world.

Why Do We Talk about Products?

What motivates people to spend so much time talking about haircuts and hotels and cell phones and grocery stores?

At least once a day, I ask someone why it is they have just told me about a product or service. What made them decide to get all wild-eyed and excited about a good book, to sneer at the price of a handbag, to recommend a pair of snowshoes, or to mention to me the fascinating fact that printer cartridges are now available in separate colors. Usually people respond to my question by saying something like, "I just wanted to tell you," or "I thought you'd be interested," or "It's such a great product, I just had to share it." But I never let people off the hook with these stock answers. I ask again, "No, really, WHY?" And I keep asking until the person gets irritated, confused, a little self-aware. (It's annoying, but it has to be done.) Ultimately, the person I'm talking with admits she isn't quite sure what made her share her opinion.

My admittedly nonscientific research has led me to the conclusion that there are six main reasons why we create word-of-mouth about products. Here they are:

Helping and Educating

This is the reason that most people would like to think they engage in word-of-mouth interactions about products and services.

It's the motivation that's easiest for people to feel good about. We all like to believe that our intentions are well meaning and unselfish. And very often they are. There are plenty of people, in plenty of situations, who really do create word-of-mouth because they want to help others make good decisions.

Helping and educating is a major reason that people get involved in the BzzAgent community. Agent daisyfay13 wrote, "Since becoming a mother, it seems that I talk about products and services with other mothers through email, on the phone, at child activities, and during pick-ups and drop-offs, and yes, even at parties. With everything to buy, watch out for, and manage, I think about goods and services all the time. I am not interested in showing off my information, but I am happy to share my information."

Proving Knowledge

But many people are very interested in showing off what they know. In our constant battle to keep up our self-image, and to ensure that others see us in the way we would like to be seen, we share information as a way of proving our worth.

For example, take my brother-in-law. Whenever he comes to visit for an evening, he always picks up at least three different rare cheeses and spends a half hour at the wine shop debating with the staff which varietals and vintages will make the best pairings for the perfect tasting. But he doesn't just bring the wine and cheese. He has to talk about it at length, describing the provenance of the cheeses and the terroir of the wines, and explaining how the two go together. By doing so, he proves to me that he truly is an expert, a maven, about cheese and wine (or, at least, more of an expert than I am). I appreciate it and certainly benefit from it, but it really does more for him than it does for me. I'm happy with a decent cab and a slab of aged gouda with saltines.

BzzAgent DontheIdeaGuy is certainly one of those who likes to demonstrate his knowledge and he's up-front about it. He most fits our original idea of the BzzAgent profile, an out-there cool guy. Don wrote, "I like the access to cool new stuff. I fancy myself a trend-watcher, so seeing the items (whether I participate in the campaigns or not) that are up for Bzz campaigns lets me add another connection to the bigger picture I am observing. I take all these bits of data and use them to create new ideas for business proposals, product and service ideas, and fodder for my writing. You just never know where a new idea will come from, and I want to make certain all my antennas are 'up.'"

Finding Common Ground

Very often, engaging in product-related word-of-mouth is an easy and efficient way to establish common ground between individuals. When you meet someone new, it rarely takes more than a few minutes to stumble onto some product or service you both can discuss. It's a low-stress way to find similar likes and dislikes, as well as a way of filling holes in the conversation. Establishing similar views is more easily done about a movie than it is about, let's say, your religious beliefs. Products and services are a handy shortcut in relationship building.

BzzAgent gprindle, a business executive, wrote, "I am one of those people who genuinely enjoys talking to people. It doesn't matter who it is. In many ways Bzzing also complements what I do. I work on deals that normally result in very large fees. I look at the opportunity to Bzz as a low-risk type of influence opportunity. Small talk is the oil of any relationship, and when I remember that a client is interested in photography (for example) and then bring up how he might want to consider Energizer®e²® lithium batteries, it improves our relationship."*

Validating Our Own Opinion

Often, we create word-of-mouth to validate an opinion we already have formed. We bring up the product just to check to see if we've missed something or if our information is correct. We want someone else to confirm that we're right.

Butman flew with his family to Florida for a few days. He called me after they'd checked into their hotel and we chatted about the trip. "We flew Song," he said, "and it was a pretty good flight. Nice entertainment system. Decent food with several menu choices. A 757. The aircraft with the best safety record of all. Have you ever flown them?"

"Why did you just tell me all that?" I asked.

"Um," Butman said, possibly annoyed. "Because you're interested in products and services."

"Why else?"

"Because I know you travel regularly. You might like to know about this airline."

"So you're sharing and educating?"

"Yes."

"No, you really wanted to validate your own opinion, didn't you?" I said. "To make sure that I didn't think you were an idiot for flying Song."

---

*Energizer®e²® is a registered trademark of Eveready Battery Company, Inc.

"Maybe. My brother flew American. My sister flew Delta. They had never heard of Song."

"Consider yourself validated," I said.

Pride

We also create word-of-mouth because we're proud to be associated with a particular product or brand. I wasn't sure that this was a widespread motivation at first, but I have been surprised at how many people feel proud about the brands and products they have included in their lives. And it's not just that they're showing them off, like status symbols, and basking in their reflected glory. No, they are genuinely proud about their choices. Patagonia wearers, Harley drivers, *Guns, Germs, and Steel* readers, Acura drivers, and wearers of Johnston & Murphy Lites. It can be any product for any person. If it feels like we've made a good decision, we're proud. Sometimes we're proud that we were able to navigate through the maze of choices and come out with a winner. Sometimes we're pleased that we made a purchase that makes our family feel safe or look good to others.

Pride is a major motivation for BzzAgents. As BzzAgent daisyfay13 wrote, "I feel an incredible sense of excitement when I see a product that I have Bzzed being sold in a store. I feel a huge sense of pride when a product that I have Bzzed wins an award, or reaches a spot on a best-seller list. To feel that you have contributed to the success of a product is a wonderful feeling."

BzzAgent gprindle wrote, "Back in high school I took one of those interest tests that is supposed to tell you what profession you would enjoy. Mine suggested I should become an ambassador, and, in many ways, being a BzzAgent allows me to be an ambassador for products."

Sharing

Finally, people create word-of-mouth because they like to share ideas, opinions, and information. There is no self-serving motive or expected result. When a product or service really makes us feel good or bad or angry or mystified, it's natural to want to share that feeling with someone else. "If I weren't a BzzAgent, I'd still Bzz about things," wrote BzzAgent SkeletonKey. BzzAgent Tatorswife put it most simply: "I love to talk, and Bzzing about products is a great way to communicate with people."

After the first Word-of-Mouth Summit in April 2005, my flight from Chicago to Boston was seriously delayed by weather. Matt McGlinn, our director of research, and I hung out at O'Hare's K2 Lounge, waiting for the thunderstorms to pass. Matt started talking about a David Foster Wallace story he was reading in *The Atlantic*. He went on and on about how no one really reads David Foster Wallace but people like to say they do. I started the process: "Why did you tell me that?" Matt is quite used to this, even though he likely still finds it annoying. After some needling, I realized that Matt did not have any particular agenda. He wasn't trying to educate me or prove how smart he was. He was just plain excited about the story, about Wallace's footnotes, and his amazing originality. He was bubbling over with the enjoyment of it, and he just wanted someone else to be part of that. We're social animals. We talk simply to connect and engage and share. It's too bad Matt chose me to talk to about the story. Instead of an interesting dialogue about David Foster Wallace and why people like to say they read him, even when they actually don't, all Matt got from me was a never-ending loop of whys.

Often the reasons we create word-of-mouth are intertwined. There are usually multiple variables at play. One reason may be dominant in one situation but not others, or at one time and not others. Listen and watch closely to your word-of-mouth interactions and you'll start to see the patterns. Be careful, though—the more aware of these motivations you become, the harder it gets to turn off.

The fact that people have personal motivations for creating product-related word-of-mouth, and that those motivations are sometimes self-serving, does not make the interactions any less genuine and honest. That's why word-of-mouth is so incredibly valuable, so real and tangible, and it's what makes it so successful in building products and services: it's honest and natural. Conversation about products is as fluid and complex and varied as conversation about anything else in the world, from global warming to sex.

A New Kind of Loyalty Program?

We hadn't figured out any of these motivations when we started BzzAgent. Sure, we read as much as we could on the subject, but most previous subject matter was about the types of people who might create word-of-mouth, and most researchers were focused on data and analysis. So, when we launched, we thought people would join the community, not just because they liked to talk, but because they could get free stuff.

That's why the original plan was for our business to be a new kind of loyalty program. Instead of receiving a credit card and spending to get airline miles, we'd get the BzzAgents involved in a word-of-mouth campaign for a client, they'd report back to us about what they were saying and hearing about the client's product or service, and we'd give the agents brand-associated rewards in return. Perks for communications.

So, we created a rewards system. The agents would receive a certain number of points for each word-of-mouth activity they reported to us. The points would accrue in their accounts. They could redeem them when they wanted to for a variety of types of swag or additional brand-associated products.

With the system in place, we were ready to go.

Our very first BzzCampaign for a living, breathing, honest-to-God client was for the Penguin Group, the publishers. (In the interest of full disclosure, let me say here that Portfolio, the publisher of this book, is part of the Penguin Group.) I had been making the rounds to every company that would listen to me, trying to get someone to believe in using our system. I called Hillary Schupf, an old friend of mine from college, and she set up a meeting with some of her colleagues at Penguin. I pitched BzzAgent to a room full of people, trying as hard as I could to avoid mentioning that we had just launched the business, had zero clients, not too many BzzAgents, and basically had no idea what we were doing. Hard to imagine, but they didn't immediately seize the opportunity to pay us vast quantities of money. At last, I offered to run a word-of-mouth campaign for them for free. Rick Pascocello, a VP of marketing at Penguin, agreed to give us a shot. The campaign would be for a book called *The Frog King,* a novel by Adam Davies.

We launched the campaign for *The Frog King* in the summer of 2002. Jon O'Toole (Jono, our communications director and the only guy who would agree to join the company . . . but only after he asked if I was sure it was legal) and I had worked for weeks creating our first BzzGuide. The BzzGuide was (and still is) a document that describes the product and outlines communication points that are intended to help BzzAgents share their opinions more effectively. We had no template to follow, no idea if any agents would actually read the thing. We didn't want it to be salesy, but it had to contain enough information so the agents could talk knowledgeably about the book. We weren't really sure what the agents would need to know to help them engage in word-of-mouth interactions. So, we mentioned several parts of the book that we thought were particularly funny or memorable that the agents could talk about. The BzzGuide was just a laser printout, stapled together. Watching it ship out of the office, I felt like a kid handing in a paper to my ninth-grade English teacher.

When the first *Frog King* report came in, we knew we were really onto something. It came from BzzAgent Jewel in Brooklyn, New York: "While leaving a friend's apartment, we were in the elevator and joking about the normal stuff. My friend Laryn asked for a book that she had loaned me. I told her I'd return the book, but then I thought about *The Frog King*. I told her it's about living in New York and had sex and a lot of drama. She laughed and said she wouldn't mind reading it because it might reflect her since she had drama when she moved to New York. When the elevator got to the third floor Laryn's cousin Keisha got on. Before I could say anything, Laryn started telling Keisha about *The Frog King*. Keisha keeps up with the latest books. She said she never heard of it but if it's about living in New York it must be a good book. They asked me where I heard about it and I told them it was the latest buzz!"

Jon and I were dizzy with joy. This was amazing. We were so excited that we wrote back a detailed response: "This is great reporting. You definitely get a big high five for this! Although we are not rewarding BzzPoints for *The Frog King* BzzCampaign just yet, we definitely wanted to show our admiration and reward you with some points. If this is any indication of the future of your BzzActivities, these will be a drop in the bucket. Keep up the awesome reporting!"

For the first few months, Jono and I answered every *Frog King* report personally, with a sense of pure enjoyment. Every report we received was another sign that the system was working.

But, shortly after we launched, we realized that things weren't going as we had planned with the reward system. Something, in fact, was seriously wrong. People were earning and accumulating points for sending in reports and sharing their opinions, but they weren't redeeming the points. They weren't claiming their rewards. We thought this might be because there weren't enough agents yet and the sample size was too small, so we ignored it. Besides, everything else about the business model was working well. Our agents were going out into the world, talking about the products, writing up reports, and sending them in. Our clients were pleased with the effect our campaigns were having on their products and businesses.

The Frog King campaign was a success. The book did well, and BzzAgent was able to attract more clients and involve more people in the network. But still our agents didn't redeem their points. We struggled to figure it out. We had heated debates, painted complex strategy maps on our whiteboard, and tinkered with the system. We sweated the details. We had middle-of-the-night epiphanies and conference calls at dawn. We finally had a hypothesis: our rewards must suck.

So, we changed the types of rewards and restructured the redemption process to make the free stuff even easier to get. We increased the number of points that an agent could achieve for each report. We lowered the total number of points needed for each reward. We changed the size of the image of the rewards on the Web site. We put up big road maps all over the Web site to point people to the rewards section. "Click HERE for rewards." "This way to REDEEM your points!" "Thanks for reporting Bzz, now get some damn REWARDS!!"

Please?

Nothing changed. Finally, during a casual chat over a game of backgammon, someone had the bright idea that we should ask the agents themselves just what was going on. We talked to a number of them directly and ran a survey on our Web site to accumulate as much data as we could. When the answers came in, we thought they must be wrong. We revised the survey questions. It didn't make any difference. No matter how we asked the questions, we always got the same types of answers. The majority of agents were telling us that they were taking part in a BzzAgent word-of-mouth campaign for reasons that had nothing to do with our rewards or prizes.

They said things like:

"I do this because I'm getting personalized feedback from brands I talk about."

"I'm finally getting appreciated."

"I like to be the first to know about things."

"It's cool to get involved with thousands of other people around the country."

DontheIdeaGuy says there are two reasons why people become BzzAgents:

1. To get cool stuff first. I think the idea of BzzAgent appeals to people who are already early adopters of new ideas. BzzCampaigns enable them to become even EARLIER adopters—to try and beat out their other early adopter friends in the unofficial game of "look at the cool thing I found before you did."

2. A sense of being "in the loop." Not so much for a sense of "belonging to a group"—which is what I would have originally guessed—but more along the lines of being on the inside of some great stock tip or knowing about a horse race or something.

Don's observations have been echoed by many, many other agents. Being involved in BzzAgent is not so much about getting the free stuff as it is about getting the free stuff before other people have it. More important, it's about being involved in a group that has inside information about all kinds of things.

But there are also agents who don't care about being first or in-the-know and have no involvement in marketing or business at all. Here's what Maria1234 says about her involvement:

"I am daring, well-educated, and opinionated. I convinced 10 friends to jump off a 50 foot bridge with me into a river. I have been to every major art museum in Europe. I drove cross country three times and saw the World Trade Center, the Grand Canyon and the largest McDonalds in the western hemisphere. I dedicated a full year of my life to community service and worked with AIDS patients after I graduated from college. I have lived on the East Coast, in the Midwest, and on the West Coast. I read banned books. I am 28 and live with 300 19-year-olds who are only slightly crazier than I am. The irony involves the amount of influence these folks have on me and on one another. When I moved to LA from Chicago, I found my optometrist, my hair salon, the local hot spots, great restaurants, and local shopping hubs by word-of-mouth. Some of my favorite bands, movies, books, clothes, and toiletries were brought to my attention by friends, colleagues, and complete strangers. I too have passed valuable information on to others without compensation. I am new to this site. However, the opportunity to read new books, try new jeans (that I really do love!!) and pass on the information that would occur naturally seems too easy. Why am I a BzzAgent? Everyone is a BzzAgent in theory. I am just lucky enough to benefit from the practice."

To this day, more than 75 percent of the BzzAgents accumulate points but never redeem them. Less than 0.4 percent have redeemed more than ten rewards in total.

The Real Rewards

In those early campaigns, we also began to realize that our responses to the agents' reports were every bit as important to them as the Bzz activities themselves. Most of them were surprised that we actually read the reports, delighted that we took the time to reply, and amazed at how much detail we put into our responses. For the first year, a good 10 percent of our agents would email us as soon as they received the first response back from us, saying something like, "Oh my god, I can't believe you actually read my report. That's so cool." Or, "I am so impressed. I thought I'd get an automated response from a machine."

We also noticed that the communication would change once the agent knew that there was a real person in our office whose job it was to read her reports. A first report might be simple and very short. Here's one from BzzAgent marju95, who was in a campaign for Johnston & Murphy Lites: "I spoke of these shoes to my dad (who travels a lot also), and then he went out and got a pair for himself."

But then, when the same agents received our responses, they would open up and the reports would become more like Jewel's story of her elevator ride. They would describe their feelings, tell their stories, and relate their experiences. It seemed that the "realness" of the dialogue between us and the agent was the driving force.

The more convinced we became that our responses were absolutely crucial to the success of the system, we made a rule: every report had to be answered within forty-eight hours of receipt and within twenty-four hours if possible. We wanted to show the agents how meaningful their reports were to us and that they were, in fact, the lifeblood of our business.

By early 2003, reports were coming in at a steady clip. We would have hundreds of them in queue waiting to be answered. Even with another communications guy, Aaron Cohen, we couldn't handle the volume of reports. Jon was whining every day. He couldn't keep up. We laughed at him. But we weren't ruthless. We enlisted the entire staff (there were a total of five of us at the time) and made a rule that everybody in the company had to answer at least ten reports a day. Not only would that enable us to better handle the volume, it would mean that everybody on staff would have a finger on the pulse of the business.

Some days we'd work until 8 or 9 P.M. in the office, then go home and spend another two or three hours answering reports. For months, I was having IM (instant messaging) discussions with co-workers late into the night, imploring them to keep going. There would be complaints. Mini-mutinies. Breakdowns. But we all agreed that this was the core of our system, even though we hadn't realized it at first. It was the engine that made everything else succeed.

As the system grew, it became blindingly clear that what the agents really wanted was interaction and communication. They would have continued communicating without the freebies. In fact, they did. In the beginning, we ran out of rewards quite often. But when we ran out of stuff, we saw very little difference in the level of activity and reporting. Agents might complain that there were no more rewards, but that didn't stop them from reporting. They continued to share their experiences and to engage in the dialogue. The tangible rewards were nice-to-haves, but they weren't what really motivated people to participate.

We found that even people who did come to our site in search of freebies often stayed because they liked the interaction. Early on, our campaigns started showing up on "freebie boards" (Internet sites where people post info and links to free offers, coupons, and other swag that is available on the Web). Amazingly enough, people who came to BzzAgent from the freebie boards apparently had a change of heart when they found out what kind of community we actually were. They came in looking for the special deal or handout, and found a different kind of passion. Just because they had a freebie-seeking side, that didn't mean they were all bad. They also had honest opinions to share. We responded to them just as we responded to everybody who communicated with us. They liked getting the response so much, their goals changed. Many of these would-be pirates emailed us to confess to their wicked ways. They admitted that they had originally joined us because of their free-stuff addiction, but ended up sticking with us because they found something much better: being involved. No, they didn't go so far as to suggest that we get rid of the points system or dump the rewards. But that aspect of the system wasn't the most important thing to them anymore.

Now that we've accumulated a vast amount of data, we know that this shift of goals is typical. About half our agents join with the intention of getting as many rewards as they can. They hear about us from a friend who got a free pair of jeans, for example, or from a posting on a freebie board or some other conversation on the Web. But once these folks get involved in the process, they realize that the product is just a small component of the bigger picture, and that the more meaningful rewards they receive are about learning, sharing, and being aware of the impact of their opinion about those products.

Over time, we got the hang of this new way of incentivizing. We learned as much from the agents as they did from us. We stopped trying to figure out how to make the reward system better and more robust. We worked, instead, to make the communications more satisfying, to make people feel even better about their involvement in the network.

We began to think of our network as one big cocktail party. Sometimes you get involved in a conversation at a party and you know immediately that the other person is just aching to move on to somebody else. Their eyes wander. They keep glancing at the buffet table. They shake the cubes in their glass. They look for an opening to say they think they'll refill their drink. But then there are other kinds of conversations. You get into a dialogue that's pure enjoyment. It's satisfying to both parties. There's laughter, no awkward moments, no scanning the room for someone to rescue you. In these types of conversations, there's a mutual respect. Something clicks, and the conversation just works. That is what we set out to create.

A new twist on a very old network: the social grapevine.

Andie, Attack Marketer

Andie is the marketing director of GlobalGajitz, a major consumer products company. She's professionally hot. Over the years, her campaigns for consumer products have generated (by her own modest estimate) six hundred million impressions. She has been featured on the cover of *Marketing Mojo* magazine. She gets a call from a headhunter at least once a week.

Andie is in charge of the launch of a promising new product, SparklyPerfect. Management has high hopes for SP, as they call it around the office. It has breakthrough features for the kitchen category. Crossover potential into the barbecue/patio segment. Could even find applications in sports/leisure and gardening/garage. It has slick Euro design with good old American ease of use.

Still, SparklyPerfect is no slam dunk. There's no product quite like it on the market, so it needs some explaining. The price point is a tad high. The big-box retailers aren't exactly sure which department to stock it in.

Nevertheless, so far, so good. Andie has completed focus groups and a limited pilot program. There have been in-store demos in selected retail footprints in three second-tier cities. A teaser Web promotion. Advertising in local weeklies and kitchen monthlies. At the stores, the limited stocks of the product have sold out. Real-time spot interviews with consumers attending the demos have shown high purchase interest.

Now the national launch is just weeks away. It promises to be a masterpiece of integrated marketing, a brilliant sequence of carefully crafted communications. It will include off-shelf displays to build awareness and trial. Market prep through national and regional lifestyle features. A burst of TV and coordinated radio. A blitz of co-op ads, outdoor and in-store events. A barrage of direct mail and couponing.

As confident as she is in the campaign, however, Andie is always pushing for that extra element, that marketing special sauce that will break through the clutter, capture the consumer, and win her more personal recognition. That's why she has placed her extra bet on a potentially breakthrough medium: taxi toppers. In cities across the country, cabs will be streaming through the streets, their roofs adorned with signs glowing with internal light. They will flash on and off as they cruise along, with each blink revealing one of three visuals in sequence: a drop-dead gorgeous product photo, followed by the twinkly SparklyPerfect logo, followed by the tagline BEYOND AWESOME!

One rainy Tuesday not long before launch, Andie meets with her boss, C. C. Farman, SVP of marketing for Global-Gajitz. The agenda: review the data they've gathered in a series of nationwide focus groups.

Andie fires up her laptop and goes to the first slide of her presentation. "SP shows high, or extremely high (in Boston, WICKED high) positives across an unusually wide range of demographics," Andie says to Farman, pointing to the multicolor bar chart. "Adults 24–49. Men. Women. Homeowners. Apartment dwellers. Suburbanites. Metropolitans. Singles. DIWKs. DINKs. Tweens dig it. Seniors want it."

"Great. But who's the PTC?" Farman asks. (PTC is Farman-speak for Perfect Target Consumer. PTC is the consumer who is most likely to buy. The consumer they must aim their message darts at. The consumer they must capture and keep.)

Andie is well prepared for the question. She advances to the next slide. "PTC is a 32-year-old female. Married, 1.3 kids. Full-time or part-time worker. Household income $50K+. Single family home on 10,000+ square-foot lot. Garage. Hot tub. Barbecue. Has visited a hair salon within the past month."

"How do we get to her?" Farman asks.

"She will have to be seriously ill, probably in a coma, or living in a hut in Death Valley to miss every element of our campaign," Andie says with great confidence.

"OK, but I mean how do we make sure she doesn't TiVo past the TV. Sirius around the radio? Put the print ad in the kitty box?"

Andie has a momentary panic attack, which she conceals by moving quickly to the next slide.

"We draw her in with the lifestyle features," she says with icy calm. "We shove the product in her face with end cappers and shelf danglers. We run a banner right through her home page." Meanwhile, she thinks: What the hell does the man want? This is a full-out campaign, as close to a sure thing as marketing gets.

Farman nods. "It's a solid start," he says, "but doesn't it all say the same thing? How do we make sure that what we're saying has consumer relevance? How do we get SP into the national dialogue?"

Andie suddenly realizes that Farman has been reading some marketing book or has come under the spell of some new would-be guru. He has always had a weakness for big new ideas that he can't wait to foist on his people.

Andie decides to challenge him. "What is it you really want, C. C.? What do you think is missing?"

Farman leans forward. "I want to get some of that genuine, honest, everyday-people word-of-frigging-MOUTH."

"Ha!" says Andie, stabbing the ADVANCE button. The next slide shows a taxi cruising along a city street at dusk, the glam shot of SparklyPerfect glowing from its roof.

"The toppers!" she says. "Who could not talk about a strobing taxi topper?"

"Let's hope you're right," says Farman, looking unconvinced. "The company has a hell of a lot riding on this launch."

He looks at her coolly. "And so do you."

3

Word-of-Mouth
Is Not Buzz

Word-of-mouth is not the same as buzz marketing or viral marketing—and it certainly isn't anything like the most evil form of marketing on the planet, shill marketing. (Shills are people paid by marketers to talk up products—both on-line and off-line—but who are not supposed to reveal their relationship with the marketer.) These methods are designed to create noise in the marketplace on the theory that if enough people hear the noise, they'll talk about it. However, what people usually talk about are the methods themselves, rather than the products. Yes, buzzing and going viral can contribute to the awareness of a product. Sometimes they're fun to talk about. But generally they don't cause people to share information, opinions, or ideas about the product, the company, or the brand that is supposed to be at the center of the buzz. They create energy around the event or method of marketing itself. They rarely deliver genuine word-of-mouth. They just cause a commotion.

Branson Buzzes Times Square

A buzz marketing activity is meant to generate publicity and excitement and, hopefully, some information about a product as well. A buzz campaign is usually predicated on the wackiest idea that a marketing team can come up with and that can be linked, however tenuously, to the product itself. These ideas have to be wacky, because buzz marketing is only effective if it's new and original.

When Richard Branson decided to launch his new Virgin mobile phone service in the United States, for example, he wanted what he always wants for himself and his endeavors—to make a huge, noisy splash. He wanted to create BIG BUZZ, something that no one would forget. The wackiest concept that he and his marketing team could come up with involved two important ingredients: Richard in the buff and a hell of a large crowd.

The idea of big buzz is to do something bigger, louder, better, more amazing, astounding, overwhelming, and incredible than the last thing you did buzzwise. Buzz marketing includes one shot of adrenaline and another shot of product information. The adrenaline helps customers forget that they're being marketed to. It also stimulates that part of the brain that registers the most primal of emotions, such as fear and pleasure, and causes memories to take hold very strongly. The information gets worked into the formula whatever way it fits.

Creating big buzz for Branson in 2003 was entrusted to U.S. Concepts, an event marketing agency based in New York. The wacky concept that Branson and his marketing partners came up with was based on the popular Broadway musical, *The Full Monty,* in which some down-and-out British steelworkers become male strippers to make ends meet. In the Virgin version, the cast of the musical would perform the climactic musical number live in Times Square. At the crucial moment when the lads strip down to the buff, who would suddenly join them but Richard Branson himself. Only he would appear on the top of a building twenty stories high. Then he would dive off the building NUDE! As he dropped, more than one hundred "red people" dressed in spandex suits would dash around, handing out product samples and information leaflets and otherwise scaring the hell out of those already frenzied commuters who were trying to fight their way through the crowd to catch their train and crane their necks upward to get a glimpse of the plunging Branson at the same time.

You know what? They pulled it off. OK, so Richard was not really NUDE. He was in a nude suit. And he didn't really dive. He was actually standing atop a giant mock-up of a cell phone and was lowered by a crane. But traffic came to a dead halt in Times Square. The guys in red spandex handed out a lot of information. Thousands of people stopped to watch. And even though a lot of them missed their 5 P.M. train, overall, it was a raging success.

What was the impact of Branson's big buzz? According to the U.S. Concepts Web site, the event "generated 150+ national media hits including *CNN Headline News,* CBS, the AP, Reuters, Knight-Ridder and Dow Jones." Not bad for awareness. The talk continued for a few days after the event, mostly centered around the crucial question: was Richard really nude? The leaflets that were handed out likely drove some buyers into stores, so consider that a success as well. But let's get our terms straight. The Richard Branson full monty Times Square dive didn't generate word-of-mouth for the product. It didn't cause consumers to share their opinion about the product or service.

All the consumer could learn from Richard Branson dropping

out of the sky possibly nude was that Richard Branson is very nervy and loves publicity. All the consumer could learn from the leaflets was that Virgin was offering a new cell phone service. Whether the calling plan was any good didn't even come into play. As usual for Virgin, branding comes first, and, in this case, it was all about Branson's package.

I still haven't heard much genuine word-of-mouth about Virgin's mobile service.

Oprah and the G6

Branson's BIG BUZZ looked pretty puny in comparison to the nationally heard hullabaloo that Oprah generated with the kick-off show of her nineteenth season on the air, on September 13, 2004. The entire season was dubbed the "wildest dream season" because, as Oprah put it, "This year on the *Oprah* show, no dream is too wild, no surprise too impossible to pull off."

Oprah promised something really, really big for the premiere, but wouldn't say what it was. She teased her audience at the beginning of the show. "You may have heard that over the next sixty minutes I'm going to do something big," she said. Cheers from the audience. In fact, the surprise was going to be so big, Oprah said, that medics were standing by backstage just in case anybody suffered a surprise-related medical emergency. Cut to shot of hunky, calm-looking medics standing by. Back to Oprah. "Let's get started," she says. More screams.

Oprah calls the names of eleven audience members and, one by one, they scurry up to the stage, gasping for air and throwing their arms around Oprah as if she were, well, Oprah. One of them cries, "I can't believe this!" as if the big surprise is just being on stage with the great woman herself. But no, that's not the secret. "You're all here because you share a wildest dream," Oprah reveals at last. Looks of delight and puzzlement. That skinny girl next to me wants to be forty pounds lighter, too? "Every one of you desperately needs . . ." Oprah pauses dramatically. Looks of unbearable anticipation. What do we all desperately need? A fridge? A vacation? No. Oprah screeches, "A BRAND NEW CAR!!!!"

Hands are clamped to heads in paroxysms of joy. Eyes roll back in disbelief. Roars of amazement rock the studio. Out rolls a shiny new sedan with a big red bow tied around it. "You're all going home with your very own new Pontiac G6! Right off the line," yelps Oprah, really getting into her half-mocking, half-serious salesmanship. Unchecked delirium.

After Oprah hypes the car for a bit and the eleven winners try to get their pulse rates under control (no medical interventions necessary, thank God), Oprah reveals that there is even MORE bigness in store.

"That was fun," she says. "But I've got a little twist. I've got one car left." Suddenly, ushers are swarming through the audience, handing out little white gift boxes with red ribbons. "There is an extra set of keys in ONE of those boxes," Oprah says. "Alright. Open your boxes. One. Two. THREE!" Audience members tear open their boxes, desperately wishing that their box will contain the keys, secretly terrified that it will not. But, to their astonishment, their box DOES contain a set of keys. Every one of the boxes. They look up, screaming with joy. Imagine their amazement when they discover that every other audience member is also holding a set of keys and screaming deliriously. "YOU get a car," shrieks Oprah, pointing at an audience member. "YOU get a car! YOU get a car!" PANDEMONIUM!

"Your cars are waiting right outside," says Oprah. "Follow me!" The entire audience surges out of the studio like a herd of thirst-crazed animals rushing toward a watering hole (you fear a bit for Oprah's safety) and discovers the entire parking lot is filled with row after row of gleaming and beribboned Pontiac G6s. Every audience member gets a brand-new, FREE Pontiac G6!

It was not just an amazing giveaway. True to form, Oprah had included an element of do-gooding in her extravaganza. Every one of the 276 people who received a free Pontiac G6 that day truly needed a Pontiac G6 or, at least, some kind of new car. It was reported that one of the winners had been driving a car with more than four hundred thousand miles on it. Another had been suffering with a vehicle that her son said, "looks like she got into a gun fight."

My oh my, what an event! What buzz! The G6 Web site was stormed, receiving 242,000 hits in the twenty-four hours after the show aired, up nearly tenfold from normal. Dealers were calling in orders to Pontiac. Then came buzz in the national media. Chatter across the Internet. Professional discussion about the genius of the *Oprah* giveaway as a breakthrough marketing strategy. The *Detroit Free Press* quoted Michael Bernacchi, professor of advertising and marketing at the University of Detroit, as saying, "This may go down in history as the lowest-cost, biggest-bang-for-your-buck product launch in the history of the automobile." The show won a Media Lion award at the 2005 Cannes Lions International Advertising Festival.

Eventually we learned that the event cost General Motors nearly $8,000,000 and that every member of the audience actually had to cough up $7,000 in tax to the U.S. government. Seems like a lot of money for both sides. But Jim Bunnell, general manager of GM's Pontiac-GMC division, disagreed. "During the Athens Olympics, GMC ran twenty-five to thirty television spots for its truck products over two weeks that cost between $7 million and $8 million," he told the *Free Press*. "But no one really talked about those ads. But the same budget, spent in one day, drove a significant amount of buzz for the G6 on a daytime television show."

The goal of the campaign was to break out of the traditional media channels and to distinguish the new car from its many midsize rivals. After much brainstorming at Pontiac, they hit on the *Oprah* idea. "We couldn't think of anybody more credible than Oprah Winfrey," said Mary Kubitskey, advertising manager for Pontiac.

But time would tell the value of this amazing event. Reports from consumers who actually drove the car and from expert reviewers weren't favorable. The *Detroit Free Press* auto critic, Mark Phelan, had problems with the G6. He gave the car two out of four stars in a review in 2004, noting, "They are attractive, comfortable and competent cars, but a high price, iffy interior and oddly tuned steering leave them well short of sporty competitors."

Everyday people seemed to have trouble with the G6, too. Everyday consumer "Athena" posted on Pontiac's G6 Forum: "Words cannot express how VERY disappointed I am with the G6. I took a test drive of a G6 GT about 2 weeks ago. It had 5 miles on the odometer. When I went to adjust the seat the power height adjustment seemed sort of loud so I asked my salesperson if that was normal (this was my first experience with a G6). She reassured me that it was normal."

But many contributors to the G6 Forum did what consumers often do when they are given a chance to participate in the conversation about a product. They made helpful suggestions about how to improve the car. "Update the engine and transmission and my own feedback is to update the door panels. Then you'll have a vastly improved sedan. That might bridge the gap between the 9,000-vehicle difference in Grand Am to G6 sales."

But it wasn't until the release of a March 22, 2005, story in the

Detroit Free Press that the truth hit about the power of this buzz event. It seemed that, as credible as Oprah may be, and as incredible as the giveaway actually was, the buzz generated by the event drove hardly any word-of-mouth about the G6 itself. Nor did it lead to a pandemonium of sales. Six months after the event, the G6 was selling fewer cars per month than the car it was intended to replace, the Grand Am, and was being offered with incentives of more than $3,600. The factory was running at 30 percent below capacity, because the demand was not there. Consumers were still purchasing more Grand Ams than G6s—almost twice as many, in fact. The disappointing sales performance of the G6 was cited as a "key reason" that Bank of America Securities auto analyst Ronald Tadross warned investors to sell GM stock in February 2005. To add to the woes, GM's overall market share went down. By April, there was talk that the Buick brand might be discontinued.

There is no disputing that Oprah's giveaway generated huge buzz for the G6. It certainly got the media and everyday people talking. But it proved once again that word-of-mouth does not follow immediately from a marketing activity. The loud noise of Oprah's buzz didn't suddenly prevent people from forming their own opinions about the car. There were, no doubt, many people who heard the buzz and who were in the process of buying a car or thinking about buying one soon. Many of them were, no doubt, perfectly open to buying a G6 if it appealed to them and met their needs. But, before making their decision about whether the G6 was a good candidate, they wanted more than buzz. They needed credibility. So, as part of their decision-making process, they went searching for real feedback from other real consumers. From their friends, their family, strangers—anyone who could tell them what the real experience was like. They went searching for word-of-mouth.

When they found it, they factored it into their purchase decision and it certainly had far more weight than the fact that Oprah had pinned the needle on the buzz meter. The irony is that a single everyday person's review—at no cost—can be more influential than $8,000,000 of advertising.

GM execs defended both the car and the unusual launch, saying it takes time to build sales and that the giveaway had created tremendous attention for the new model.

Millions of people had seen the wildest dreams Pontiac G6 giveaway on *Oprah*. Millions of people had talked about it to millions more. But there was a huge gap between how the marketers were talking about the car and how people were talking about the car. People were talking about how cool it would be to win a free car—but not THAT car.

The Subservient (Viral) Chicken

Viral marketing is quite a different animal from buzz marketing. Its method is to manufacture a marketing message, almost always online, usually in some tangible form such as a video clip or an email, that can spread quickly and exponentially among consumers. It usually has some off-beat, mysterious, bad-taste, or anarchical component to it. These are the messages you receive from that friend in Seattle who has too much time on his hands and sends it to all four hundred people in his address book, with a subject line that reads something like, "Thought you might find this amusing," or "This is very cool."

In 2004, the subject line might have been "the subservient chicken." This was a viral marketing campaign developed in 2004 by Crispin, Porter + Bogusky for its client, Burger King. The task: to promote BK's new Tendercrisp Chicken Sandwich.

Typing "subservientchicken.com" into your Web browser, you would find a low-budget-looking video with a man dressed in a low-budget chicken suit standing in a low-budget living room. (Lord knows, he may be there still.) You could make this poor chicken do all sorts of (low-budget) things simply by typing your command into the bar below the image. I admit, I made the chicken do the funky dance. I made him smoke a cigarette. I tried to make him vomit, but for some reason the programmers hadn't included that particular capability.

It's true, I visited the subservient chicken site a number of times. I emailed the URL to friends. Then I emailed the page that included all the keywords about what the chicken would do. I talked about it with many people, and shared the concept of the chicken with them. The chicken was addictive. It was viral. It got shared all around the world.

The problem is, the chicken did not create any more genuine word-of-mouth for Burger King or its chicken sandwich than did the nude Branson for his mobile phone service or did the breathtaking *Oprah* giveaway for the Pontiac G6. The viral chicken created word-of-mouth for the subservient chicken and the site and the weirdness of viral movies. After I made the subservient chicken smoke a cigarette, did I make an irresistible connection between the low-budget chicken man and the allure of the Burger King Tendercrisp Sandwich? I did not. Did I mention Burger King's amazing new chicken sandwich to other people? Nope. Did I think about McDonald's french fries? Possibly.

In fact, according to *Hitwise,* it seems McDonald's Web traffic increased more than Burger King's did during the time the Burger King subservient chicken campaign was clucking along in full force.

The subservient chicken was viral marketing at its finest. It may have increased the overall brand perception of BK (now they're cool, some may think), but the chicken was a one-trick chicken-pony. The missing ingredient: word-of-mouth.

The Village of Deception

Both viral and buzz marketing are manufactured marketing initiatives that are intended to capture people's attention and get them talking.

Viral ads can be effective at cutting through the marketing-advertising clutter, but when they become pervasive, they are at risk of becoming part of the noise or worse. Some marketers, in an attempt to get the dialogue going, try deceptive means to get their consumers to go viral. But this is like playing with matches. It can backfire and cause negative word-of-mouth, as evidenced by the M. Night Shyamalan brouhaha for his 2004 movie *The Village*.

The story goes that Shyamalan agreed to participate in a documentary film to be produced and aired on the Sci-Fi Channel, and directed by Academy Award–nominee Nathaniel Kahn. The film would be a profile of the mysterious supernaturalist Shyamalan (he of *Sixth Sense*) and would take the viewer onto the set of his new movie, *The Village*. But, supposedly, during the four months that the filmmakers trailed him, Shyamalan often became unhappy, would fail to show up for interviews, or would cut off the questioning in the middle of an interview. At last, Shyamalan withdrew from the production altogether, but the relentless filmmakers fearlessly continued with an "unauthorized" portrait, even though M. Night threatened them with a lawsuit. The Sci-Fi Channel leaked the story of how badly things were going to the Associated Press, which wrote a story and delivered it to its huge network of media contacts. The story was out.

Publicity for the three-hour movie, which was called *The Buried Secret of M. Night Shyamalan,* hinted that the filmmakers had discovered a terrible, dark secret about M. Night and that it would be revealed, despite Shyamalan's protests, in all its hideous glory. But, two days before *The Buried Secret* was to air, the Sci-Fi Channel got nervous about whether it had pushed things a little too far and whether there might be a backlash. It sent out a promotional clip from the documentary and tried to tip off the press that all was not as it seemed, by saying the film was more "mock than doc." This did not have the desired effect. It just added to the story.

Finally, the Sci-Fi Channel spilled the beans. The whole thing had been a hoax, it said, a "mockumentary." Shyamalan had been in on it all along and his withdrawal was just part of the fiction. The channel had intended that his shocking secret (something about a boy, a drowning, a small town) would go viral. The press was outraged that it had been used. Sci-Fi issued an apology. It was just a guerrilla marketing campaign that had gone too far, the channel said. "We never wanted to hurt the press," said Sci-Fi spokeswoman Jean Guerin. "We did this type of thing before and our viewers expect this from time to time. . . . We were looking to play along with our brand and it's something we worked on with Night." But Sci-Fi did do something right. It came clean before it duped every single fan of the channel and of M. Night's work, alienating them forever.

Like the phony reviews that are often posted by authors' friends and enemies on amazon.com, this attempt at creating positive word-of-mouth through a totally fabricated event devalued the entire conversation and made its developers look bad. The word-of-mouth was not about what a great filmmaker Shyamalan was or about how cool his new movie was sure to be, it was about what a stupid prank they had pulled. And how easy it was for them to misjudge their audience.

The Value of Transparency

As hard as marketers have tried to generate genuine product word-of-mouth through buzz and viral marketing efforts, they haven't had much luck, because so many of these efforts are obviously manipulative and often have little, if anything, to do with the values of the product itself. People are not that stupid. And they hate to be fooled.

When the buzz activity is clever and everybody knows the rules of the game, however, it can add a little zip and awareness to the brand. Besides, it's not as if buzzing is a new idea. One of the most obvious and venerable buzz marketing activities is the one recognized by every reasonably alert, bar-hopping college student. He knows very well that the trio of blondes sporting Swedish accents and far-too-tight T-shirts who chat him up as they clutch bottles of Bud in "wazzup" beer koozies and offer him a free one are, in fact, in the employ of Anheuser-Busch. Their chitchat about the beauty of Bud is perfectly harmless and their professed interest in their Perfect Target Consumer (PTC) and his delightful sense of humor are understood by all to be totally, 100 percent baloney. Everybody knows the game. No harm, no foul. Live a little. The buzz generated by these interactions is short-lived. "I got a free beer from a babe in a T-shirt." The word-of-mouth is inconsequential.

But many companies have conducted buzz campaigns in which the PTC does not understand the game or only sees the rules after he has been suckered. This can sometimes work, but more often backfires.

In 1999, Vespa decided to venture where no marketers had ventured before. It devised a campaign based on a stunningly insightful bit of social analysis: that people will respond positively to other people who (a) are attractive and (b) appear to have an interest in them. Vespa recruited a squadron of yuppie hipsters, both male and female, and paid them to ride the city streets on Vespa scooters. When the scooter-riding shill spotted a likely Perfect Target Consumer, usually at an outdoor café or some other public location, he or she would veer to the curb and strike up a conversation with the usually unsuspecting dude or dudette in question. There would be flirting. There would be double entendres. There would be sly references to current cultural ripples. And there would inevitably be chat about the visiting hipster's ride of choice: the hot-painted, pimped-out, chrome-studded, perfectly polished toy of joy, A.K.A. the Vespa. It wasn't as blatant as the Bud girls. As a matter of fact, it wasn't blatant at all. The scooter did not sport any overly conspicuous Vespa branding. No Nalgene bottle with Vespa logo. No bomber jacket with scooter embroidery. No wraparound shades with Vespa gators imprinted in six-point font. It was possible for the Perfect Target Consumer to convince himself or herself that this chatting hipster was a Vespa lover who, for some unknown but wonderful reason, had just taken a shine to the PTC. So far, the target consumers were completely in the dark about the intentions of the Vespa riders, but nothing harmfully phony had been going on. What happened next was where it went wrong.

After much cooing and lavishing of attention, the Vespa hipster/model—imagine that: good-looking shills—gives the Perfect Target Consumer his or her phone number or email address. Score! The disheveled, overweight, unshowered guy cannot believe his luck. He cannot wait to get home to call his soon-to-be girlfriend.

He speeds back to his pad. He taps in the phone number. He waits, barely able to breathe, as the phone rings. What does he hear? An automated phone voice, asking him to please hold for the next Vespa representative who will gladly help him choose the right Vespa model for his individual needs. He hangs up, resists throwing the phone against the wall, tries the number again, and gets the same hatefully automated and uncaring voice. Some of the more even-tempered PTCs, especially those who already have a girlfriend or boyfriend (or both), find the hoax slightly amusing. Many others are annoyed, angered, embarrassed, or even ashamed they have been so easily duped.

A couple of years later, Sony Ericsson mobile took the Vespa idea a big step further and created a campaign that can be considered a watershed moment in the history of alternative marketing. (Ericsson partnered with a number of advertising and marketing agencies on the campaign. This story need only be read by the three marketers in the universe who haven't claimed to have had some hand in it.)

Ericsson's goal was to introduce its new mobile phone, the T68i with picture-taking capability, to the average consumer. The phone-as-camera was still very new, but the advertising clutter in the mobile phone space was unbelievably dense. Ericsson would have had to spend megabucks to reach its Perfect Target Consumers and, even if the company did make the spend, it was not convinced that the mass media initiatives would actually pay off in sales. So Ericsson's marketing team came up with a very special marketing sauce. They hired a squadron of sixty actors and set them loose on the streets of six U.S. cities. But it deployed them more cleverly than either the Bud girls or Vespa deceivers.

One team of Ericsson actors dressed up like ordinary looking tourists, complete with maps and fanny packs, and vapid gazes at civic attractions. They took themselves, in groups of two or three, to popular tourist spots, such as the Empire State Building in New York and the Space Needle in Seattle. When the Ericsson "fake tourists" spotted a Perfect Target Consumer (who could be almost anybody), they would approach and ask (sometimes in charmingly "I'm-not-from-around here" English) if the PTC would be willing to take their picture. The friendly consumer would, of course, oblige. Then came the beautiful moment. One of the fake tourists would reach into his multipocketed cotton-poly travel jacket and pull out—not the point-and-shoot camera that the consumer was expecting, but an Ericsson cell phone. A look of pure awe would pass over the unsuspecting consumer's face as the fake tourist showed him how to take a picture with the phone. Conversation ensued. The consumer asked questions and made comments. The fake tourists followed, more or less, the Ericsson script. Message darts were carefully thrown. Consumer objections were easily dealt with. But the fake tourists, with equal care, did not mention that they were in Ericsson's employ. They didn't even get to keep the phones once the curtain on this particular performance closed.

A second team of Ericsson actors fanned out to trendy bars and happening eateries. They would make and take calls on their T68i phones, which would display the image of the person on the other end of the line. Others would take up positions at the bar some distance from their partners and play battleship on their phones.

The campaign got results. There were many conversations between the fake tourists and the real consumers. Those conversations spawned many more, rippling out in generations with word-of-mouth about this very cool phone that could also take pictures. The street encounter had meaning. The consumers got to try the camera. They heard the messages within the context of a "real" experience. They made a connection between the product and the person.

But, as effective as the street experience was, it was the public relations attention that really made the campaign. The press had a field day reporting on this new medium. Most called the campaign ingenious. A few journalists took the trouble to interview some of the consumers who had taken pictures of the actors. Most of them were intrigued by the whole gig. But many were peeved. They felt sullied. Taken advantage of.

In October 2003, *60 Minutes* ran a story called "Undercover Marketing Uncovered," which featured a segment about the Ericsson campaign. It included comments by John Maron, Sony-Ericsson's marketing director. "That was an easy way to create a very noninvasive interesting conversation with somebody without the pressure of it feeling, like, this is a pitch," he said. "In a sense, it was easy for the people to just fit into the area in which they were." But Malcolm Gladwell, also interviewed for the piece, said, "There's a set of rules that govern a lot of advertising and we're aware of the rules. We're aware that the woman in the advertising for Ivory Soap is prettier than most women in our lives. A line is crossed, I think, when you go outside of those normal boundaries and start to deceive people in ways where they are totally unwitting to what's going on."

A lot of companies were willing to cross that line, but many of those followers found it difficult to deliver the results that Ericsson had achieved. Nissan thought it would be a good idea to have actor-moviegoers stand up in movie theaters to shout out poetic phrases along with a Nissan commercial running before their favorite feature. People may have laughed at the commercial about the "rude cell phone guy," but they were freaked out by these standing troubadours. Unlike the cell phone encounter, which—despite the fact that it was contrived—at least resembled a real-life situation, the Nissan trick was unbelievable and ridiculous. What kind of fool would sing along with a commercial in a movie theater? The Nissan piece received a few mentions in the press, but mostly from reporters scratching their heads about who could have thought up such a harebrained idea. There were plenty more such forays into "undercover" marketing, but few worked, because they didn't get any coverage at all.

Without transparency, these attempts to create word-of-mouth are fruitless. Over time, the consumer gets hip to them and is able to easily spot the phony Vespa driver, fake tourist, or paid theater singer. The press finds it less and less interesting as a new take on marketing, and will gradually find more news value in the negative results.

Good Viruses and Bad

The first person who told me about *The Blair Witch Project* was my brother. The low-budget film was supposedly created from the footage of three student filmmakers who went into the woods to make a documentary and never returned. A year later, their footage was found and, from it, the freaky film was made about vanishing children, a curse, and witchcraft. My brother told me that what had happened in the movie really had happened, which he knew because he had heard that it was true from a "friend in Maryland." The action of the movie takes place in Blair County, which is located in north-central Maryland. I guess my brother figured that a Maryland resident would be a reliable source about the state of witchcraft and documentary filmmaking statewide.

When my brother learned that the whole thing was a hoax, however, he was not outraged. He thought it was funny and interesting. No one had ever experienced anything like *Blair Witch* before. Of course, the subject and style of the movie fit perfectly with the covert marketing approach. It was all underground, mysterious, deep-in-the-woods, nobody-knows-for-sure stuff. If the same thing had been tried with a different kind of movie—

say, *Armageddon*—it would have flopped. (Forget about the acting performance of Ben Affleck. Combining him with asteroids just isn't close to believable.)

It's interesting to note that, although there was a *Blair Witch* Web site, most of the word-of-mouth about the movie was face-to-face. (Remember, 80 percent of word-of-mouth takes place in live dialogue and only 20 percent online.) But, the huge success of *Blair Witch,* a movie that reportedly cost about $30,000 to make and grossed about $250 million, spawned a slew of copycat viral online campaigns. A short underground movie appeared on the Internet, in which a cat tiptoes across the trunk and up onto the roof of a Ford, then falls into the sunroof, which closes unexpectedly and decapitates the creature. Not funny. Not clever. Not word-of-mouth worthy. As irrelevant to the product as the subservient chicken was to BK. Ford and its advertising agency claimed that they had nothing to do with the grim little movie. Must be those kooky consumers acting up again.

Online viral campaigns get in trouble primarily when their creators assume that people can be fooled and will not guess who is really behind the action. If Ford had created the campaign knowing that its name would be associated with the viral video, the company never would have risked offending the legions of cat-loving car owners and dozens of animal activist groups such as PETA. But, because it was covert and, supposedly, the company would never be linked to it, Ford thought that it could push the limits. That was a case of very poor judgment, like naughty boys making silly anonymous phone calls to strangers, thinking they'll never get caught.

One of the more notorious examples of nontransparent viral backfiring came in early 2005, when a viral ad, which appeared to be for Volkswagen, started circulating on the Internet. We see an intense man at the wheel of a VW Polo, driving hard through the streets of an unidentified city, which does not appear to be in the United States. He approaches a café where several tables are filled with lunchers. They glance up at the Polo as it swerves to the curb and stops. Inside the car, the man reaches for an ominous-looking button that nestles between the front seats. He pushes it. From outside the car, we see a violent flash of light. The man, we suddenly understand, is a terrorist and the button is a detonator. The car windows have gone opaque in the blast, presumably because they have been coated with the bodily effluents of the exploded terrorist. But the exterior of the car remains intact, the lunchers go on eating, and a tagline appears: "Polo. Small But Tough." The viewer realizes that the ad is meant to demonstrate how strong and well constructed the VW Polo really is. You can blow up a bomb inside it and, after a little interior clean-up, you're good to go.

The company now is always the first suspect when viral wrongdoing is suspected. In a sequence of events that has become almost routine, Volkswagen and its agency of record, DDB, first publicly disavowed the terrorist spot. Then the creators of the spot, a British boutique agency called Lee and Dan, came forward to claim responsibility. According to one source, Lee and Dan revealed intimate knowledge of the spot and how it had been made. It had been shot on 35mm film, for example, which is expensive and not easily available to amateurs and rarely used for Web media.

Lee, of Lee and Dan, apologized for the spoof spot, which he said was not meant to be released on the Web. He also declined to say who funded the spot, which was estimated to have cost some £40,000, which is peanuts for a television spot but a lot for an amateur Web prankster.

"We made the advert for Volkswagen," said Lee. "We never really intended it for public consumption. It was principally something we made to show people in the industry, but it got out somehow." In other words, the ad seemed to be a promotional demo for the agency that it had made in hopes of getting work with VW. Or anybody with a very dark sense of humor.

By late January 2005, Lee and Dan were feeling the heat of their in-bad-taste-but-may-get-VW-and-the-world-to-notice-our-small-agency trick. VW threatened to sue the agency. People found themselves talking about VW and the Polo and the ad. But mostly they were talking about how bad it was. They were wondering why the idiots who made it would stoop so low to get attention and hoping that the whole thing would bring the agency down. Lee and Dan had gained fifteen seconds of viral fame in exchange for their dignity.

The fake Polo ad shows how dangerous the viral advertising game can be. There is so little accountability for what appears online, it's easy for almost anyone to toss a message in any form onto the Web and watch it proliferate almost instantly without anyone knowing its original source. This anonymity emboldens people, companies, and noncompanies to push the limits of acceptability. The line that separates getting noticed and being hated has gotten very thin.

The problem with these viral tactics is that, like Branson's buzz-making experiences, people don't pay attention to the ones that don't create a visceral reaction. To create word-of-mouth about a viral ad, you have to do something that people love to talk about. That usually means sex, political or social humor (such as the Jib/Jab site featuring animated versions of presidential candidates Bush and Kerry singing their opposing versions of "This Land Is Your Land"), or evil and violence—or, of course, gross-out jokes. But, like the subservient chicken, most viral advertising creates word-of-mouth about the ad itself, not about the product. Sure, you may get some heightened awareness, but you may not have gained credibility. In fact, you may have lost some.

Does the ability of a VW Polo to withstand a terrorist blast translate into a feeling that the car is of sound construction and makes you feel safe? No. It makes you think that the filmmaker thinks we're fools.

These viral ads also show just how little control there is over anything on the Internet. Although nobody can have absolute control, everybody can have a little control or at least some influence. That means that anyone who wants to make a name for himself can take advantage of brands on the Internet in ways they cannot in other media, including print and television. But the kind of shock and awe required to gain attention at the expense of a brand is a one-time deal. You can't do shock and awe twice. Viral ads are fads. They don't create lasting impressions. Few create word-of-mouth about themselves. Few create word-of-mouth about the product or brand. People talking about the attributes of your product or brand does.

This is not to say that online viral campaigns never work. They can. They can even be elusive and mysterious, so long as it is obvious to the viewer that the mystery can only be the work of the marketer. The Honda "cogs" campaign is a great example. The spot is an ingenious piece of mechanical wizardry, in which the parts of an automobile interact in a Rube Goldbergesque way. The sequence is begun when part A does B and causes part X to do Z, and on and on, as the camera tracks along with the action, with each part's movement causing the next action in the sequence. The only sound in the spot comes from the movements of the parts, as they roll and spin and touch and tap each other. At last, an entire car is revealed and the movement of the final part causes the car to roll down a ramp, at which point, the Honda logo appears. The spot had Web browsers transfixed in front of their screens for the entire two-minute running time, not knowing what the spot was about, because it was so beautifully made and so wonderful to watch. People madly emailed the spot to each other. Honda's new model was subtly introduced. Nobody was deceived. No cats were decapitated. It was effective, well-intentioned, transparent virality.

Ah, but how can a viral campaign that is designed to be transparent continue to be transparent as it moves from one person to the next? Even if the company, or the evangelists, that develop a campaign make it known who they are and how they're involved, how can that transparency be maintained when they are no longer directly involved with the viral spread of their work?

The solution is in the nature of word-of-mouth. If transparency is embedded in the viral campaign, as it was with the Honda cogs campaign, then consumers will continue that transparency. It's only when the marketer's intentions are devious or unclear, as with *The Village,* that a viral campaign gets in trouble.

Now, maybe if we got Oprah into a chicken suit and made HER do the funky dance, we'd really have something to talk about.

Or maybe not.

Launch Day

Launch day for SparklyPerfect arrives!

Andie does not sleep well the night before. In fact, she has a weird dream. In it, Farman is holding a book, but Andie can't discern its title. Standing behind Farman is a gauzy figure, a dark-haired young guru. Farman opens his mouth and his voice sounds like it's from a bad 1950s movie: "How do we achieve consumer RELEVANCE with this thing?" his voice booms. "How do we get SP into the national DIALOGUE? How do we get word-of-frigging-MOUTH?!"

Andie wakes up drenched in sweat. She suddenly realizes that Farman is right. Maybe, as much depth and reach as the campaign has, it will just be another bunch of messages lost in the great clutter. She leaps out of bed. It's not too late to do more.

Meanwhile, in his second-tier city in another part of the country, Bardo is also up and at 'em. By the time he hits the floor of the dairy department, he has been exposed to ninety-seven marketing messages, including four about SparklyPerfect. There is a four-inch display ad among the forty-six ads he half-sees in his two morning newspapers.

There is a fifteen-second TV spot among the seventeen commercials that air on the five channels he flips through. There is the SparklyPerfect billboard that he glimpses out of the corner of his eye. There's also the SP radio spot whose tail end he catches while switching between Howard, Imus, NPR, and weather radio.

Four little message darts have been thrown and they have hit their target. Four impressions for Andie to track. Four impressions for Farman to calculate into his ROI. But, for Bardo, they have not made much of an impression at all.

Bardo spends the morning working the milk-and-cheese case, then meets with a couple of folks from the International Dairy-Deli-Bakery Association (IDDBA), who are visiting from out of town. After a tour of the department, Bardo takes them to a new sushi place for lunch. On the way, they whiz past a cab with the flashing SPARKLYPER-FECT taxi topper. But it isn't flashing because the light isn't working. Nobody notices it.

At lunch, after talking about baseball, Mexican cheeses, freezer technology, kids, and cell phone usage plans, one of the guests mentions an interesting new gizmo that she has seen advertised and wonders if anybody has heard about it.

"What's it called?" Bardo asks.

"SparklingPerfect," she says. "Something like that."

"I'm aware of it," says Bardo, realizing that he knows virtually nothing about it. "It looks pretty good," he says lamely, and changes the subject to the new HotFinger™ freezer mitts with built-in temp gauge.

By 9:30 A.M. Andie has assembled her team in Spock's Den (A.K.A. Conference Room 1). She addresses her team with urgency. "We've done a good job on Phase One. The messages are out there. Snaps all around. But have we gone far enough? Are we being proactive enough? What ties it all together?" She looks out at blank stares.

"Specifically," Andie continues, "are we doing enough to create BUZZ? Are we doing ANYTHING to create buzz?"

Silence in the room. Somebody says, "What is buzz exactly?

"Well, now's the time to figure that out," says Andie, realizing that she is not exactly sure what buzz is or how to create it. "I don't want to leave this room until we've come up with some killer ideas for stimulating buzz or word-of-mouth or whatever it is that we're missing."

An hour later, the whiteboard is a catastrophe of marker scribbles. The buzz-making ideas include:

- PERKY SQUIRREL CHARACTER RIDES COMMUTER TRAINS AND HANDS OUT "WALNUTS" IMPRINTED WITH SPARKLYPERFECT LOGO.

- VIRAL VIDEO IN WHICH SPARKLYPERFECT ARM WRESTLES A CONVENTIONAL KITCHEN BLENDER .

- WRITE ROMANCE NOVEL WITH TORRID LOVE SCENES IN KITCHEN. INSTEAD OF SMOKING CIGA-RETTES AFTER SEX, LOVERS USE SPARKLYPERFECT TO MAKE ROMANTIC DINNER.

In the end, they all agree on the Perky Squirrel character. There's just something very in-your-face and impossible-not-to-notice about it. It's sure to get attention. And why wouldn't people love a squirrel? They loved the Budweiser frog, didn't they? And the Aflac duck? Besides, the company can execute on this strategy fast and cheap. Hire some actors. Rent some squirrel suits. Print up some walnuts. Bingo.

The only question is whether the squirrels can create what Farman wants: that good, ol'-fashioned, regular-folk, word-of-frigging-mouth.

About that, Andie is not so sure.

4

How Word-of-Mouth Proliferates

Think of the consumer as a big round grape.

Think of that consumer living on a vine. With a bunch of other grapes.

Now picture an entire vineyard. A mass of vines all tangled up with each other.

There's the consumer-grape you want. It's that dark purple one, out there in the middle of all those impenetrable roots and shoots and tendrils.

You could shout a catchphrase at the grape. The grape might hear it. But it might ignore you.

You could also say something to the nearest grape to you, that pinkish one. Mention to it that the dark purple grape in the middle of the vineyard would probably be interested in what you've just said.

The pinkish grape will start talking.

You can't tell if the pinkish grape is on the same vine as your deep purple grape, but it doesn't matter. All the vines intertwine. You know that they'll eventually intersect with each other.

However, you can't control exactly what route it will take.
Or what kind of grape will ultimately deliver the message.
Or whether the message will be repeated just as you said it.
Or exactly how long it will take to get there.

None of that matters. The grape is far more interested in what other grapes have to say than it is in catchphrases shouted from a distance by message purveyors.

The grape will listen. It trusts the other grapes. It wants to interact with them. And, soon enough, the entire vineyard will have heard the message.

Generations of Word-of-Mouth

Just like a message traveling the grapevine, word-of-mouth reaches its target consumer indirectly.

In a BzzAgent program the individuals who first share their honest opinions are classified as generation zero (Gen-0). We choose Gen-0 people based on certain characteristics or demographics, then let them experience a product and help them understand how to communicate the experience more effectively. We help them form an opinion—which doesn't always have to be positive—and enable them to talk consistently about it with others. That may mean getting a free sample. Like a pack of Energizer®e²® lithium batteries or a copy of *All Marketers Are Liars*. It may mean receiving a coupon to redeem at the store. Or it may mean descriptions, images, and a potential free trip to Prague with ACIS, the educational tour organizer.

We describe to the Gen-0 people what kinds of other people are likely to be most interested in the product and their opinions about it. But they are free to talk to others as well. You never know who will be hanging out with whom.

The campaign begins, and the Gen-0s begin to interact. From the reports of their activities, we know how many people they are interacting with. A word-of-mouth participant has, on average, five to seven interactions about a product or service during the course of a twelve-week campaign. That may be fewer than you expected. But these people have lives. They do not spend every waking moment Bzzing products. And they wait for appropriate moments to do so. Marketers may want there to be more interactions, but more may not bring about any greater result. Five or six or seven genuine, honest word-of-mouth interactions may be more powerful than five hundred advertising impressions.

From the Gen-0s' reports, we also get an idea of who the Gen-1s are, but the information we collect is anonymous. All we know is that the Gen-1 is a "guy at work" or "my mother-in-law" or a "woman I met on the plane."

From the reports we also learn how the Gen-0s interact with the Gen-1s, and how the Gen-1s respond. We learn about where the interactions take place. How the product figures in the interaction. What is communicated. And what the result is, if there is one.

Then the grapevine opens up into its beautiful, tangled expanse. The Gen-1s carry the communication along the vine, without any control or monitoring by us. They decide how to communicate about the product and whom they communicate with. How word-of-mouth proliferates from Gen-1 onward is entirely in the hands of the consumer. To realize the power of this medium, the communication must not be controlled or managed.

This is a scary thought for the marketer. How can we ensure that the Gen-1s don't screw up the message? How can we be sure that they'll talk to the right people? How can we know what the hell is going on out there?

Here's how: We make sure that our original communication

with the Gen-0s is entirely genuine, honest, and worth talking about. If we do that, the communication between Gen-0s and the Gen-1s will also be based on honest opinions as opposed to marketing taglines. If a Gen-0–to–Gen-1 interaction is credible, then the interactions that follow on from it are likely to be credible as well. However, if the original interaction is disingenuous, incredible, dishonest, phony, or deceptive, then all the interactions that spring from it will be just as deceptive. But consumers will seek out the truth. If it doesn't jibe with what they're hearing, all word-of-mouth about that particular product or service will then be suspect, and will need to gain more and more credibility before a purchase can occur.

Not only is the progress of a message through multiple generations untrackable, there should be no attempt to track it. But companies try and will continue to do so—with member-get-a-member promotions, multilevel marketing, couponing, coding, and requests for return of information. All of these efforts are attempts to follow the word-of-mouth message trail. But these efforts damage the pureness of word-of-mouth. As soon as a person is asked (or required) to do something that forces her into a control mechanism, the data becomes corrupt.

Word-of-mouth has to be allowed to proliferate naturally. Or else, by definition, it isn't word-of-mouth at all.

You Talkin' to Me?

As word-of-mouth proliferates across the generations, interactions will inevitably take place among many different kinds of people, in different communities, and not all of those people will fit the profile of the target consumer, because the reality is that you are never sure exactly who will eventually touch the target consumer. It could be almost anybody. You may reach people who, even though they don't fit the profile, actually are interested in the product. You might, in other words, find new audiences.

BzzAgent neejla, a member of the campaign for Energizer®e²® lithium batteries, had a word-of-mouth interaction that no one could have predicted. "I had to stay after school for a club I joined, so at four I got on the bus to go home. This old woman sat next to me and kept watching everything I did. I was listening to my CD player and the batteries went dead, so I took out a fresh box of Energizer®e²® lithium batteries. She was amazed. She turned to me with her mouth opened and asked, 'Is that the kind of battery you young people are into?'

"I couldn't help laughing before I said no. I explained to her that there are various kinds of batteries and that nobody really cares about who's using what batteries, it just happens that I like lithium batteries. She wasn't satisfied and turned to me and said, 'Well then, why would you buy that kind of battery? They are too expensive, compared to other types of batteries and they do the same thing.'

"Once again I laughed and told her that they aren't really the same because lithium batteries last much longer. I was surprised that this woman, who looked to be at least 60 years old, paid attention to the price of batteries. Then she asked me to let her listen to my CD player. I was just stunned. I told her that I didn't think she would like it. But she was persistent and said that that was the silliest thing she had ever heard of. The rest of the ride she was listening to my CD player and moving her head like she was some teenager. When my stop came and I got up to get off the bus, she gave back my CD player and said, 'I have a feeling that you were being honest when you told me about the batteries and I think I'll buy a pack for my granddaughter.'"

No marketer would have put these two people into the same category. The sixty-year-old woman would have been off the radar. But, she helped the word-of-mouth message proliferate across communities, from the community of Teenager on the Bus to the community of Granddaughter.

Word-of-mouth isn't bound by geographic or regional constraints either. Communications frequently occur in regions where consumers reside together, but sometimes—in today's connected, global world—it's quite the opposite. BzzAgent Taralynne wrote, "What a small world! I was flying out of LAX airport to go home for Christmas when my flight was delayed for 7 hours. What to do? I struck up a conversation with a guy waiting for the same flight. Turns out we went to the same high school and had common friends, although we had never met. (Even graduated the same year!) By the time we boarded the plane 7 hours later we were like old friends and by coincidence were seated next to each other! Fate maybe? So I'll get to the Bzz. . . . We shared a common taste in music. We were exchanging CDs and listening to them simultaneously on our separate disc players when his battery died. He was bummed but I had two more of my sample e^2 lithium batteries in my backpack and knew I wouldn't need them as I had just put them in my own disc player. I gave him the batteries and told him about how he should switch to them so that he can listen to his music longer next time just in case I'm not around. He had never heard about them and asked if they were expensive and where he could buy them. We intend to keep in touch after the holidays so I'm sure I'll be able to check up on that later."

Traditional marketing often targets people by geography. But we live in a global, boundaryless world. We interact with people in communities all around the country. We email, phone, and IM. We go to trade shows. We read books from other cultures. Newspapers and print information from other regions. We gather data that is regionless. Businesspeople talk more often with clients in distant cities and random seatmates on planes than they do with their co-workers back at the office. Interested in targeting Dallas? Maybe you should consider communicating with individuals who went to college there or spent five years working at a company there or have a sister who lives there.

Segmentation parameters are still valuable, but we need to recognize their limits. Just because I bought my printer in Boston doesn't mean that I made the decision to buy it there. In fact, it was the interaction I had with a guy in Poughkeepsie, who had just spoken to a colleague in Seattle, that put me in the know.

The Pass-Along Effect

When word-of-mouth proliferates from generation to generation, across communities and geographies, it's interesting to note what individuals consider worth communicating about. One of the most fascinating elements of word-of-mouth is that we are constantly seeking to share information. We like to know. We like to be known for knowing. We like to have an opinion. This is why we sometimes share information about products that we have no firsthand knowledge about at all.

This idea of sharing information without any firsthand knowledge is what we call the pass-along effect. People hear things about a product or service and, at some point, they start passing along what they've heard to others, just as if they had experienced the product themselves. A real person—even one who has no direct experience—brings more credibility to the conversation than a perfect marketing message does. Sometimes the person who's passing along the information makes it clear that he has no direct experience with the product. He'll say, "I haven't read it. But I've heard it's a really good book." Sometimes, he won't be so clear. He'll just say, "Oh yeah, that's a good book." Even the most scrupulous of us, those of us who think it's wrong to tout a book without having read it or a movie without having seen it, now and again find ourselves fabricating slightly. It's just a tiny step from "I hear it's really great," to "It's really great." When you hear a similar opinion about something enough times from enough people, it's hard not to digest it and transform it into your own. You're not lying. You're just telling a slightly different kind of truth based on an indirect kind of product knowledge. The odd thing is that we actually believe these opinions just as much as the ones we form through direct experience.

At some point, we consider that our opinion has been "formed" about a product, simply because we've heard enough about it from enough people, whether or not they have any direct knowledge of it.

Remember Wacky Packages from Topps? They were available starting in the early 1970s. They were sticker packs with goofy parodies of real product packages. For example, instead of Wheaties, the Breakfast of Champions, the Wacky Package was for Weakies, Breakfast of Chumps. There was one for Rice-A-Phoni instead of Rice-A-Roni. Others were for Crust toothpaste, Cap'n Crud cereal, and Crackola crayons.

One fall day, Jon O'Toole dragged me to the Brimfield antique fair, the largest gathering of antiques sellers and buyers in New England. We wandered between rows of makeshift booths looking at rickety wooden chairs and other knickknacks for hours and hours. It was fascinating, but unproductive—until I stumbled into a booth where someone was selling the original press run sticker tear sheets of Wacky Packages. A flood of nostalgia washed over me. I just had to have 'em. Forty dollars later and I was the proud owner of my very own tear sheet. (No one told me I was supposed to haggle at these fairs.) I paid three times as much to frame it, and now it hangs on the wall of our office.

The tear sheet's value for word-of-mouth engagement is enormous. Everyone who sees the tear sheet starts reminiscing. There's a moment when most people see it and you can see them thinking: Where have I seen these before. And then the light bulb goes on and they say, "I remember these!" Usually people start chatting about their youth and how they used to collect them; many folks bring up Garbage Pail Kids, the esteemed leader of the "offensive sticker" era, and many folks rattle off a personal experience with Wacky Packages. Sometimes people mention the one or two that are their favorites and then wonder aloud if anyone still makes these things.

Often enough, an even more interesting dialogue occurs when one of our younger staff members happens to be around when a Wacky Packages conversation is in progress. The staffer engages in the dialogue in almost exactly the same way as does the person who grew up with Wacky Packages. One of our co-workers was a toddler when Wacky Packages originally came out, but he's usually the first one to engage with others about them. He'll talk about which one is his favorite. He'll crack up about them when others do. And, if the conversation happens to be with a visitor who has never had the glory of encountering Wacky Packages before, the guy will get excited and explain everything about them: when they came out, how they were sold, how kids used to collect them. Often he accidentally forgets to mention that he only found out about them when we hung the tear sheet in the office, not in 1973 when the stickers first came out. Why? He feels good about passing along knowledge that comes from experience. But that knowledge and experience really comprised the collective opinions of others who have remarked on the tear sheet. He would pass along our opinions in a manner that made them his own.

The pass-along effect isn't quite as brainless as it sounds. People do not repeat just anything they've heard from anybody they've heard it from. People begin to believe others' opinions and embrace them as their own only under certain circumstances, including when they:

1. hear the same or similar opinions about something often enough that they feel they have a "preponderance of evidence." If enough people say it, it's likely to be true.

2. receive feedback from a person they trust or whose opinions about certain categories they trust. "I like him, and I like many of the things he likes, so I'll probably like this thing, too."

3. don't want to appear ignorant about the subject.

Any of these circumstances can lead a person to form and pass along an opinion about a product or service he has no direct experience with or knowledge of. When two or three of the conditions exist, the person is likely to feel even more strongly about his indirect opinion.

Consider the story of BzzAgent heatherzilla:

"I went to see my father for the holidays, and my aunt from Detroit was also visiting. My father is a recent widower and complained as he was making us some coffee about how it has been hard being alone since the death of my stepmother. He said that simple things like making coffee bother him. It reminds him of their morning routine. I asked him if he ever heard of the Home Café System where he can make just one cup at a time. My aunt said that her friend in the Detroit area has one and loves it. My dad never heard of it. My aunt said that's it, you are getting one for Christmas. She headed to Wal-Mart and came back within an hour with my Dad's Christmas present, a new Home Café System and pods. He loved it. He told my aunt that it was the best present he ever got."

Neither woman owned the Home Café System nor had either one tried it. But there was sufficient evidence to seal the deal.

To test this for yourself, open any newspaper to the movie list-ings. Pick a page and circle the ads for movies you have a positive opinion of in one color, and circle the ones you have a negative opinion of in another color. Now, for all of those you circled, write next to them what you're basing your opinion on: a review, actor/actress, trailer, a recommendation, general word-of-mouth, or actually having seen the movie yourself. It's likely that you'll discover that you have no direct experience with the majority of the ads you circled.

Then take a look at the ads you circled because you'd read or heard a review of the movie. In most cases, your opinion will be in sync with that of the reviewer. You have borrowed the reviewer's position and used her experience and knowledge as your own. You may have many good reasons to believe and trust the reviewer, but it's still not your opinion that you're expressing. You've made an in-formed guess, and just having access to what you perceive as the "right" information is enough to create that opinion.

The pass-along effect can result in people sharing all kinds of misinformation and having fairly half-baked conversations, but it can also have another result. Very often, when people hear in-direct information, or pass it along themselves, it stimulates them to gain direct experience.

We learned about this in our early campaigns. Due to the time it takes for a package to be delivered by mail or delivery service, there is often a lag between the moment when an individual in our system joins a campaign and when they receive their BzzKit (which includes various ways to experience the product and in-formation about how to share their opinion most effectively). In the first campaigns, as people joined our system and had no idea what to expect, we would receive very few reports about word-of-mouth activities during that lag time.

But, in early 2004, as more individuals began to understand

and have expectations of the system, we began to see a dramatic change in behavior. In many campaigns, there was almost no lag time at all between the moment people joined and their first report. People would join a campaign and within hours—minutes in many cases—begin reporting their activities.

What was happening? BzzAgents who had been accepted for a campaign, but had only heard about the product from us, decided not to wait for their BzzKits to arrive before they started Bzzing. They were so eager to get involved with certain kinds of products, they couldn't wait the week or ten days it would take for the package to arrive. Instead, they'd research the product online, go to a store to check it out, ask friends if they had tried it, then use their knowledge to begin creating word-of-mouth. Many of them actually went out and bought the product that they would be receiving free in a few days, just so they could learn enough to talk about it with others. BzzAgent had become a source of pass-along information. It didn't matter that we hadn't given them anything. We had given them, in essence, a "tip."

The first time we saw this in a big and convincing way was in the campaign for a new fragrance from Ralph Lauren called Ralph Cool. Here's what an agent in Clemson, South Carolina, reported:

"This Bzzz campaign was made just for me! I began Bzzing before I even joined! I was at Macy's Herald Square in NYC and I saw a girl at the perfume counter giving one of her customers a sample of the new Ralph Scent: Ralph Cool. Now I've been a huge fan of the original Ralph perfume so you can only imagine my excitement at the prospect of an updated version! I went straight to the counter and asked the salesgirl about the new scent. She told me that it had just barely hit stores and gave me a sample of the perfume; it came on a postcard and was a small patch of material saturated with Ralph Cool. It was like Christmas! I knew I'd only be able to use the sample once so I decided to wait to open it until I went back down to college (in South Carolina). The postcard was burning a hole in my pocket and the first night that I got back to SC from my trip to New York, I went to my neighbor's house for a get-together. It was a warm welcome home and after I told them the details of my trip I exclaimed that I had a surprise to show everybody! I dug my postcard sample out of my purse and we all waited in anticipation as I opened it! I dabbed some of the sample on my wrists and it was love at first smell! I shared the tiny sample with the rest of the girls who enjoyed it just as thoroughly as I did! The only disappointment was that the sample was gone and we wouldn't be able to wear it come morning. On the upside, one of the girls promised to buy a bottle soon and she gave us her word that she'd share!"

However, not all agents are quite so scrupulous. Many are so willing to take our word for a product that they are even less inclined to seek direct experience before they start talking than they might be otherwise. A BzzAgent from Walnut, California, for example, didn't bother going to the store or doing any research at all:

"I was soooooo excited to see a campaign for Ralph Lauren that I immediately called my friend after signing up for the campaign, and I asked her if she had heard that Ralph Lauren was coming out with a new fragrance called Ralph Cool. She said 'really?' I said 'yeah!' Her favorite perfume is Ralph Lauren Romance, so I knew she would be really excited to hear about it. She said 'If it smells great like Romance I will have to get it.' I told her that I was getting some to try and she was so jealous. I told her that I would let her know how it smelled and would let her try it so she could give me her opinions. I also sent her a BzzAgent card to sign up for the campaign. I will definitely let you know what she thinks of the scent! :)"

An agent in Maryville, Illinois, got the whole office buzzing about Ralph Cool just by going online for a look:

"After signing up for the campaign I went to the website for Ralph Lauren. While looking at the site a co-worker stood over my shoulder and was interested in what the fragrance smells like. I started explaining about it & how I would have some to let her smell in a week or so. She was so excited she ran around the office bragging about the new campaign I am working on. Others from the office came to hear about the fragrance & who makes it, where it can be bought, how pretty the bottle is, etc. Bzzing is so easy."

The Ralph Cool campaign taught us that BzzAgent had become, in effect, a source of pass-along information. We provided the indirect experience that allowed the consumers to identify with the product and share an opinion about it with others. Their acceptance into the campaign, and the expectation that they would be learning more about the product in the near future, was more than enough to get them talking with others about the fragrance. They didn't claim that they knew more about the fragrance than they did, but simply because they were closer to the brand (through their relationship with BzzAgent), they felt empowered to start their Gen-1 interactions. Imagine how fast the word rippled through the generations in that campaign.

Through a poll of the agents involved in the campaign, we learned that nearly 10 percent of them bought the product before their free, full-sized bottle arrived in the mail. They trusted that if we were doing a campaign for a product, it was worthy of word-of-mouth. What's more, they felt so good about being involved and embraced by the brand that they didn't want to wait to engage.

The Word-of-Mouth Window

It takes time for a message to proliferate throughout the grapevine. Because of the naturalness of word-of-mouth, it's impossible to say how long it will take for the message to get from one person to another. But there is usually a window of time during which communication moves across generations most naturally and easily. This is what we call the word-of-mouth window. After running more than a hundred campaigns with tens of thousands of consumers, we've found that the average word-of-mouth window for most products is about twelve weeks. We know that three months is about the right amount of time for a word-of-mouth campaign because we've run others that were too short and some that were too long. The optimal length of time may vary slightly for different products and services, but it is rarely very much longer or shorter.

Our early book campaigns were just eight weeks long. We learned that many people tend to start talking about a book very early in their reading, when it's freshest and most intriguing.

Even so, we found that the reports came in slowly at first, built gradually, and then surged dramatically in the first few days of the final week of the campaign. The volume of activity and reports increased through the very last day of the campaign, as people tried to meet the eight-week deadline to communicate with everybody in their networks. The window we offered BzzAgents was too short. So, in the case of book campaigns, or campaigns for other products that require some time to understand, the window obviously needed to be longer.

When we lengthened the running time for book campaigns to twelve weeks, the results were much stronger. BzzAgents didn't have to rush to create word-of-mouth or attempt to manufacture opportunities to spread it, both of which make the conversation less genuine. They could take their time to influence their networks.

In 2004, we decided to fully test this premise. We wanted to understand exactly how long people would talk about books if there were no restrictions on their campaign involvement at all. So, we decided to extend our book campaigns for an entire year. We knew that books can take time to find their audience. People don't always buy a book immediately, even if they hear about it and think they might like it. That's because they're already reading something else, or they're in the mood for mystery at the moment rather than a business book or a chick lit novel. But a month later, or six months later, they're looking for something to read and are open to word-of-mouth about what they should try next. The problem is that a publisher actively markets a book for only about five weeks after launch.

Rick Pascocello, VP of marketing at Penguin, and I thought it would be smart to extend the campaigns for the eleven books we were working on. The marketing directors at Penguin thought it was a great idea, too. They don't like abandoning books that might eventually find an audience, but they usually have no choice, considering the pressures of the business and the market. So the extended word-of-mouth campaign seemed to them to be a good value, a way to increase the number of impressions per marketing dollar. Turns out, that was traditional marketing thinking about a nontraditional marketing approach.

We found that the year-long campaign unfolded just as if it were a three-month campaign. After the first twelve weeks or so, the word-of-mouth activity slowed down. Some books kept people talking a little longer, some a little less long, but every book flatlined long before the year was out.

Although there is a window, that doesn't mean that individuals will stop communicating after it closes, just that the bulk of their dialogues and interactions will take place during that time. This is partly because people seem to be able to sustain their interest in a new product for a limited period of time. It's also because we're all constantly juggling several products in our word-of-mouth portfolios. There are only so many products and services we can interact with at any given moment, and only so many communications we'll have about them. Some products become a priority to communicate about, while others are discussed only when someone requests information or if something triggers a conversation. Either way, the word-of-mouth list is short. The products you talk about heavily today are likely not the products you spoke about a year or even six months ago.

And that's how it works on the grapevine.

A message proliferates in an unpredictable sequence that has a predictable result.

Every grape in the entire vineyard hears the message—not from some recorded voice bellowing at them from afar, but from the source that influences them the most.

A fellow grape.

Who's Your Maven?

Not long after launch, Farman calls Andie into his office.

"We're not meeting target," he says. No expression on his face. "Six percent lower than plan."

"We're only two weeks in and we've passed breakeven," says Andie, trying to keep Farman from going haywire. "We haven't launched the second wave. Direct mail hasn't even gone out yet. This stuff takes time to work."

"Feels like a short-term increase to me. Do you think people are really understanding the product?" Farman asks. "Are we talking to them enough?"

Andie looks Farman straight in the eye. He is not going to derail the campaign with his premature ROI jitters. "Maybe it's a longer sales cycle than we thought," she suggests. "Or maybe it's that nasty price point." Although the price had tested well, Andie had thought that it was too high, and had battled against it, to no avail. "Or maybe," she said, not willing to let Farman second-guess her masterful campaign, "there's just so much clutter out there for so much crappy product that we'll have to spend more than we thought to break through."

"Maybe," Farman cuts her off. "But I think we still don't have what we really need."

"I know, Buzz!" Andie says decisively. "We're working it. We'll have the concept ready for review next week." She does not quite have the stomach to tell him about the Perky Squirrel character.

"Good," says Farman. "But it's not just any old buzz we want."

"No?" Andie sighs. Farman obviously has read another chapter of the guru's all-knowing tome.

"No," says Farman. "Buzz is no good unless it has credibility."

"Right," says Andie.

"And where does credibility come from?" Farman asks rhetorically.

Squirrels? Andie wonders.

"Credibility comes from INFLUENTIALS," Farman says.

"Influentials," Andie repeats.

"Yes," says Farman. He gestures eloquently with his hands. "We need mavens."

It is at this very moment that Andie decides she needs help. If Farman wants to capture the PTCs, generate honest and genuine word-of-mouth, create buzz WITH credibility, and set loose a flock of mavens, the Perky Squirrel character likely won't cut it.

Farman grabs a book from his credenza and hands it to Andie. "You might want to read this," he says.

"It's by the man they call Word-of-Mouth Pilgrim. Perhaps you should give him a call." Farman hands her the guru's business card.

Andie's fingers are trembling as she dials the number. Then, lo and behold, the WOM Pilgrim himself answers. He is aboard a plane, waiting for takeoff, but is never too busy to talk to someone who wishes to engage in dialogue about word-of-mouth. Andie explains her problem.

"What you need," says the Pilgrim, "is real PEOPLE! People talking about your product. People who will share their ideas about SparklyPerfect with others. Show it to their friends in their homes. Take it out on the deck and hold it high for all to see. Mention it during the staff meeting at work. Take it to show-and-tell at school."

"And how do I get them to do that?"

"You create a word-of-mouth campaign that dovetails with your other marketing efforts. You reach out to ordinary people who are interested in your product. Give them the opportunity to become part of your brand. To become evangelists. There is nothing more powerful."

"How?" asks Andie, not at all sure how to go at this. "And what's it going to cost?"

The Pilgrim chuckles. "Sorry. We're taking off. Gotta go."

Meanwhile, Bardo catches a ride home with his co-worker, Cam. Bardo throws his bag in the backseat of Cam's new hybrid and notices a large shopping bag there.

"What'd you get?" Bardo asks Cam.

"This new SparklyPerfect kitchen thing," Cam beams, with a touch of superiority.

"Oh, yeah. I know about that," says Bardo. Cam and Bardo carry on an understated competition about who is most in the know about new products and services. "It's a little pricey, isn't it?"

"Maybe," says Cam. "But it's great quality."

"How do you know?"

"My sister got a prerelease version on eBay," says Cam.

"Are you going to use it to barbecue?"

"You need a special accessory for that."

"Oh," says Bardo, seeing an opportunity to go one-up on Cam by getting the full barbecue-ready SP. "How much did it cost?"

"$87.95 after a $10 mail-in rebate," says Cam.

"I got a 20 percent–off coupon online," says Bardo, with a sly chuckle.

"I checked that out," says Cam, deadpan. "You can't use it in-store. And it's only good for selected colors."

Point and set to Cam. Damn.

That night, Bardo tells Megan that Cam has bought a SparklyPerfect. Megan has also heard good things about SP from one of her clients. The barbecue is only a couple of weeks away. Why not go for it?

Bardo goes online. Feeling that guilty little thrill that comes from taking the plunge on a new product, he ticks off the boxes for:

Product:	SparklyPerfect
Quantity:	One
Color:	Crushed Pepper
Accessories:	Barbecue StorageMate
Delivery:	Two-day (extra charge)

Bardo wants to tell somebody about the new purchase, but Lily has gone to bed and Megan is working on a design project and is not to be disturbed.

So Bardo sends an email to Cam. "Bought a SparklyPerfect," he writes. "Got the barbecue accessory."

Point for Bardo?

5

The Myth of the Influentials

If only Oprah would mention SparklyPerfect!

Or Martha.

Or what about Jack? Either Jack (Nicholson or Welch) would be great.

Or how about Serena or Lance or Tiger?

Failing them, what about an expert in the category? A maven.

Or, perhaps, just a very connected person. Someone with a huge network. A sneezer. Or a bee. A trendspreader.

Stop!

Word-of-mouth from celebrities, mavens, connectors, alphas, hubs, transmitters, trendsetters, whatever-you-want-to-call-thems is always good. But it's no more powerful or influential than word-of-mouth from that guy with the weird headphones who was sitting next to you on the train or that gal you dated over one summer.

I know how tempting it is to believe in the myth of the influentials. It's so clear. So easy to explain. So salable. "All we have to do is get the right people on our side. They'll talk up the product.

The masses will listen. Sales will follow like sunshine after a thunderstorm."

But what if your product is breakfast cereal or stone walls or socks? Who is the sock connector?

You're not alone. When we started BzzAgent, we believed in the myth of the influentials. It took nearly a year of campaigns and thousands of interactions with BzzAgents for us to understand that mavens and high-profile influentials are effective in specific ways and in particular categories, but that most of the time, everyday people are better. They are the ones who are having word-of-mouth interactions that generate results—creating awareness, changing perceptions, and driving sales. They're the ones who make and break products and services every day. Ask yourself, when was the last time you were influenced by an influential? Not recently, I bet. Most of your interactions are with people who wouldn't be classified as special networkers. But you listen to their recommendations anyway.

Personally, I haven't spent a lot of time with Oprah or Lance. But I do interact with my family, the gang at the office, my friends, clients, partners, service providers, the guy across the street at the coffee joint, the lady at the baby shop. I'm not sure if I could identify a cool kid or a trendhunter if I tripped over one. I don't associate with Japanese thumb tribes (known as oyayubizoku in Japan) or run with an underground network of cyberthieves. I'm pretty ordinary, really.

But you may not be. Perhaps you do fit the profile of an influential or alpha. Maybe you do a lot of volunteer work and have a huge network of people you talk to. You adopt products earlier than the rest of us. You know how to speak three languages. You have a knack for making friends. But listen closely. You probably don't influence any more people than the rest of us do. It's OK.

Even if I did hang out with either Jack, I doubt that his opinions about cars or snowshoes or wine would carry any more weight with me than anybody else's.

The simple fact is that people are always influenced more by other people than they are by anything else. Hearing about a new product or service from another person, even if that person has no particular influence or expertise at all, even if you don't like that person or they're kind of slow, has more influence than hearing about it from a television ad or a Web site. Just the act of a living, breathing person choosing to speak about something to us is meaningful.

Who's Really under Whose Influence?

Celebrities and mavens are easy to identify, but everyday people with influence are less so. How do you know who's going to wield the most influence with a target consumer about a particular product or service?

In 2003, we partnered in a study of word-of-mouth marketing led by two academics: David Godes, assistant professor at the Graduate School of Business Administration at Harvard, and Dina Mayzlin, assistant professor at the School of Management at Yale.

The goal of the study was to test the idea that word-of-mouth generated by certain individuals is more influential than word-of-mouth spread by others. We particularly wanted to see if it was the opinion leaders and fiercely loyal customers, the people who generate the most word-of-mouth, that have the most influence on others.

The study was based on a word-of-mouth campaign we ran for Rock Bottom Restaurants Inc., a national chain of brewery restaurants. Rock Bottom introduced the BzzCampaign by email to a few thousand members of its Mug Club loyalty program. The members had been invited to join up and, as a reward for their involvement, received a discounted meal and other loyalty program perks.

Rock Bottom's Mug Club is like many other loyalty programs. Members receive a card to use at the restaurant that enables them to win rewards and prizes. They receive their own "specialized" mug (always awaiting them at the bar) and get invitations to special dinners and beer tappings. Ten visits earn them a Mug Club baseball cap. Fifty visits earn a Mug Club BBQ set. After fifty visits, every ten additional visits get the member $10 in "club cash" spendable at the restaurant. If you quaff 120 pints, your name will be immortalized on a plaque. The attraction of such programs to the company is that the members can be easily tracked. Rock Bottom knows exactly who is visiting the restaurant, how often, at what times, on which days, as well as how much they spend and what they buy.

We used two criteria to select Rock Bottom Mug Club members for the BzzCampaign: the loyalty level in the Mug Club program, and the number of visits they made to the restaurant on average each month. We divided the participants into three groups: light loyals, medium loyals, and heavy loyals.

About four hundred Rock Bottom Mug Club members chose to participate, the great majority of whom were light and medium loyals, along with another six hundred current Bzz-Agents who were not Mug Club members. We were pleased at the interest in the campaign, but we were surprised that more of the heavy loyals hadn't gotten involved. Why wouldn't they want to talk about the brand that they were obviously so passionate about?

We identified two Mug Club heavy loyals in particular who seemed like naturals for the campaign. Dwight from Denver had bought 1,812 pints of beer over 476 visits. Rodd from Tempe was another heavy loyal, with 1,360 pints purchased in 427 visits. These guys were obviously big fans of the restaurant, especially its brewery.

At last, Rodd from Tempe broke down and signed on. Almost immediately, about sixty other heavy loyals joined him. But Dwight, king of the loyals, was a holdout. We couldn't understand why a guy like that wouldn't want to be involved. Rock Bottom seemed to be his home away from home, a place as dear to him as his hometown ballpark. I imagined him showing up at Rock Bottom just like Norm did at Cheers, a frothing beer waiting for him even before he settled onto his specially reserved bar stool. How the hell could Dwight not join? How could such a loyalist be so disloyal?

I should have realized that Dwight's reluctance to join was not a weird anomaly. It was a clear expression of a fundamental aspect of word-of-mouth influence. But we couldn't see what was going on with him yet. We just kept hoping he'd join.

The campaign began and the reports started coming in. Again, we were surprised. Although Rodd and many of his fellow heavy loyals had joined the campaign, they didn't contribute much. Rodd did not send a single word-of-mouth report during the entire campaign. Val from California, who had visited his favorite Rock Bottom restaurant nearly one thousand times, sent in just one report. Same for another heavy loyal, Glenn from Phoenix.

But this was not the case with light and medium loyals. Brooke from Chicago, BzzAgent Suprgrl379, was a light loyal who had visited a Rock Bottom restaurant just three times and had drunk a relatively modest seven pints of beer while she was there. But she filed a total of six reports, more than the average for the Rock Bottom agents.

In her third report, she wrote, "On Thursday, 4/3, my fiancé and I went to Rock Bottom for dinner. I, of course, filled up on those Titanic Toothpicks* (I can't seem to get enough of them!) and could not finish my pasta. So I decided to bring my leftovers to work the next day for lunch. And on the way out, I grabbed a menu and threw it in my bag. The next day, I went to take my box out of the bag and there was the menu! I had forgotten to take it out at home! So I left it on my desk. While I was eating my leftovers, everyone in the lunch room kept commenting on how good my meal smelled. They even kept asking for bites!!! I did let a few people have a taste but I had to put a stop to that. Otherwise I wouldn't have had anything left to eat and, besides, I get a little greedy when it comes to food from Rock Bottom! Anyway, I told them where it was from and they all expressed interest in going there soon."

When we were running the Rock Bottom campaign, Bzz-Agent had only a handful of employees, and we all spent the majority of the campaign with our heads down, trying to manage and respond to the reports that were flooding in. I'd occasionally check in with Dave Godes, who was helping us with the tracking and measuring. But there wasn't much for him to do while it was running, so we spent our long days and nights answering Bzz-Reports from passionate users—no matter how many Titanic Toothpicks episodes they told us about or how many ! and :-) marks they felt compelled to use.

When the program ended, Professor Godes and his team went into action. They compared the agents' reports with Mug Club member data to see if there were correlations. They tracked sales and visits for each participant as well as for the program as a

---

*Titanic Toothpicks are, according to the Rock Bottom Web site, a "delicious combination of smoked chicken, Jack cheese, and seasonings stuffed into rolled tortillas, fried golden and topped with guacamole, sour cream, and fresh salsa." Mmmmm.

whole. We looked at the level of Bzz activity of each participant. We looked at their report activity in detail, including how many people they had communicated with in each activity. We evaluated the effectiveness of their communications. Did the communication cause other people to visit the restaurant? Was anybody motivated to join the Mug Club?

After about six months of work, Professor Godes sent me a massive spreadsheet containing more data than I thought could be gleaned from a humble BzzAgent campaign. He left me a cryptic voicemail saying that the findings were "very interesting." When we finally spoke, it was clear we'd learned something completely unexpected.

Overall, the campaign had been a raging success. First, we looked at restaurant sales data for the six months before the campaign started, and the projections for how much revenue would normally be created by the loyalty program without the help of a word-of-mouth campaign. Then we compared these figures with the actual sales data. We found that in the first three months of the campaign, the Mug Club program had an increase in trending sales of about $1.2 million above trend. What's more, the average frequency of visits increased 37 percent, the spend per visit went up 12 percent, and the number of members signing up for the Mug Club card also rose by 55 percent. Not only did the program cause current Mug Club members to get more active, it also motivated them to bring in more new members than they had previously, simply by sharing their own enthusiasm with others.

OK, so the campaign worked. And it was measurable. Wonderful news. But the most intriguing insight was the one that David Godes found lurking deep within all that sales data. He discovered that the heavy loyals, the major Mug Clubbers, weren't the ones whose behavior was changed by the campaign. The Rodds and the Dwights of the Rock Bottom world were not especially interested in getting involved in a word-of-mouth campaign that was designed to help the company they seemed to care so much about.

Why? There are many likely reasons. Professor Godes thinks that heavy users have done their talking early in their relationship with Rock Bottom. They've already told their friends and colleagues and family members and acquaintances. Everybody knows the heavy loyals are heavy loyals. There is nothing much more for them to say or anybody left to say it to. The heavy loyals have passed through their personal word-of-mouth window.

I believe there's another reason as well. The heavy loyals have gone beyond an interest in the brand and have entered a state of "personal brand ownership." For the guy who has drunk 1,500 pints at his favorite Rock Bottom, the place has become a second home, a clubhouse, a part of the personal landscape. He doesn't really want to tell others about it, because he feels some ownership of the brand. He's a product narcissist. He feels that he has become an important member of an exclusive club and his name on the 1/2 Barrel plaque is proof of it.

In any exclusive society, in order for there to be "insiders" there must be "outsiders." The more "inside" you get, the less willing you are to open the door and invite others in. In fact, you're more likely to shut the door and go entirely quiet. Why risk wrecking a good thing? Why threaten your own status? Why involve yourself with a marketing campaign designed by outsiders and intended to bring more outsiders in? While it's likely that some individuals who reach this nirvana of beer peanuts continue to influence others, it's clear that many don't.

So, the heavy loyals, in a formalized word-of-mouth campaign, may not be your best participants. They may be just the people to send direct mail or make a special offer to. They might show up for Two Pint Tuesdays. They might buy more, and more often. But they might be talking less than you think.

When we wrapped up the campaign and started analyzing other campaigns we were running, we were better able to characterize the three types of loyals.

The heavy loyals are completely committed to a brand, product, or service. These people will listen a lot and take advantage of offers and invitations. They really don't mind being thought of as targets of the brand. In fact, they enjoy it. They may or may not be big talkers and generators of word-of-mouth.

The medium loyals are the true brand evangelists, people who are the most vocal and communicative about a brand. They like to be the first to know. Evangelists add a great deal to the conversation. These are the experts who often know more about the product than most people in the product company do. They're the people who develop convincing ways to talk about the product that are different from the official marketing messages. They know how to "sell" it in a genuine fashion and handle other people's objections. Most of all, they demonstrate to others just how important the product is to them. They are the ones who are constantly adapting and learning about the brand. Changing their opinion and their identity to embrace the brand as an outspoken participant.

The light loyals are happy to buy a product and patronize a company, but they don't spend their days pondering the brand. These people, as we saw with Rock Bottom, are the ones who are most likely to generate effective word-of-mouth. They have networks that can be influenced, and are seen as believers but not evangelists. (Evangelists can be so overwhelming in expressing their opinions that they turn people off.) The light loyals are the consumers who should be embraced through dialogue, rather than just through promotional offers, discounts, and rebates.

They can be very valuable and become true insiders who are willing to listen and then share opinions both with the company and with other consumers.

But let's not forget the professional experts. What influence do the restaurant reviewers and the culinary mavens wield? We found that restaurant reviewers, many of whom had already reviewed their local Rock Bottom, were not particularly interested in reengaging with it. A restaurant reviewer gains influence and authority by being ahead of the curve, by being the first to try the new place and the first to identify the trends that relate to all things hot and steamy. Once they put their words on paper, they must move on. Many reviewers joined the campaign but didn't really engage. They'd seen this movie before. They'd told others about the Titanic Toothpicks. They had a byline in *Zagat*'s. They had been quoted on the back of the menu. If they were asked about the restaurant, they surely would have given a strong opinion. But proactively talking would be like taking a step back in their career as an expert.

Then there are the experts who are friends and foodies. The buddy who enjoys the finest duck roulade, and knows the sommelier well enough to chat with him about how the kids are doing in college. Or the pal who adores greasy ribs and a fine pint, and can tell you how much sugar has been used in the barbeque sauce. Part of their identity is based on their mavenism about where to eat and what to eat when you're there. They may have a favorite joint, but outside of that, it's rare that they'll go out of their way to recommend the same place twice in a short period of time. These people had little effect on additional sales at Rock Bottom either.

The lesson is that the most influential communicator for an established brand like Rock Bottom will probably not be the person you would expect it to be. It is not the heavy user or the passionate loyalist. Nor is it the recognized "opinion leader"—the influential—the pundit, reviewer, or expert. You can buy a celebrity product placement if you want someone "cool" to be seen using your product. But creating real dialogue? Leave that to the regular folk.

The most influential person in a word-of-mouth campaign like the one we did for Rock Bottom is the person who takes interest in the product and is positive about it but does not feel so personally attached to it (or even personally defined by it) that he can't share. It was the light loyals who were the most influential talkers in the Rock Bottom campaign and drove its sales results.

Many of the light loyals were motivated by an interest in helping the brand. They felt recognized. They liked being listened to. They felt like ambassadors for good old Rock Bottom.

When's the last time Apple called you to thank you for introducing the iPod to everyone on your street?

Talking to the Wrong People

Determining who has influence over whom can be more complicated in some communities than it is in others. Sometimes the communities who are interested in your product are influenced by people drastically different from them, or part of another community that operates within their sphere of influence.

We've noticed this in many of the campaigns we've run over the years. One of the most interesting instances of this was in a campaign we developed for ACIS Educational Tours. These folks develop, organize, and manage trips abroad for high school students—say, twenty kids in Amsterdam or Paris or Rome for a week of education and museums. And coffee shops. And gift shops. This type of trip can be a tremendous experience for a high schooler. They can also be very disorganized and disappointing. So the choice of tour organizer is important.

It's usually the high school teacher who initiates an educational travel program, after learning about the opportunity provided by a tour organizer such as ACIS, which offers to organize and run it. If enough students sign up for the trip, the teacher travels free, courtesy of the tour organizer, and may get other delightful perks as well. Overall, the system works. The kids get a special experience abroad. Parents feel assured that their kids are in trustworthy hands and doing something educational as well as fun. The teachers get some good travel out of the deal.

After September 11, 2001, ACIS, like many other travel organizations, experienced a serious drop in business. Fewer teachers were willing to lead trips. Fewer parents wanted their kids to travel abroad. Business did not bounce back as quickly as ACIS had hoped. By the end of 2003, it was looking for new ways to increase the number of trips. Its marketing efforts through traditional media channels were not generating the results it wanted. The company figured word-of-mouth might be worth a try.

ACIS came to us and asked us to develop a word-of-mouth campaign. It wanted only agents who were teachers. It believed that teachers needed to support each other and that their communication about previous trips would be a catalyst for new teachers to consider a trip. Teachers who had run a trip, or even those who had not yet run a trip but had investigated running one, could share the knowledge they had gained about ACIS. Word would spread from teachers' room to teachers' room, from school to school, from town to town. Pretty soon, the phones at ACIS would be ringing off the hook.

But who was really helping these trips come together? Although the teachers are the ones who initiate the trips, they are not quite as all-important in getting them going as it appeared on the surface. For a trip to come together, the school administrators have to approve it. The kids have to get excited about the destination and about the teacher who will be leading the journey. The parents, who are the ones who are going to open their wallets and come up with the bucks, need to have faith both in the teacher and in the tour organization. So, although teachers undeniably are instrumental in the process, when it came to running a campaign, we became less and less convinced that they are the ones who have the most influence on each other.

We discussed our concerns with ACIS, but the company continued to express its belief that teachers were the best influencers with other teachers. They were the experts in educational travel, after all. ACIS's data showed that parents and students do not play a substantial role in the development of programs or in the selection of the travel organizer. The teachers are the ones who have influence with all the constituencies, including other teachers. Getting parents or students involved in a word-of-mouth campaign, our client told us, was just "not going to work." Hell, what did we know? Our instincts told us that, at best, the teacher community might be too isolated to successfully create word-of-mouth and, at worst, they wouldn't have enough influence to get positive word-of-mouth going with others. But we didn't have any formal research to tell us otherwise, and we certainly weren't experts in the educational travel market. Besides, we were young and needed the business. We went ahead.

Initially, we had some difficulty getting teachers involved in the campaign. Some of them said that they didn't want to participate because they had already had an experience with ACIS and it hadn't gone as well as they had hoped. (However, I doubt that the number of unhappy customers was any greater for ACIS than for any other travel organizer. They were just more visible because they were being asked to actively communicate and get involved with the company.)

But, as the campaign developed, we realized that there was another reason that teachers were reluctant to participate. Most of them didn't want to be put in the position of trying to exert influence over other teachers. They didn't mind generating word-of-mouth about the experience of the trip itself—where they went, what they did, what worked, and what didn't. But they did not want to talk with their constituencies about how they created, developed, and managed the trip. Why? Because they didn't want to undercut their own efforts in developing future trips. With limited numbers of kids in a school who could or would take a trip, and only so many trips a school can run, there is a limit to how many teachers can fill a trip. Teachers were afraid of their competition: other teachers.

However, even once we filled the campaign slots with teachers, the word-of-mouth still didn't take off. And it wasn't because of the friendly competition among the teachers. It was because the communities that really influenced the teachers about overseas tours weren't part of the campaign. The real influencers were the students and parents. The students talk up the planned trip to Italy to other kids. They tell stories about how much fun they're going to have, how much pizza they're going to consume, and whether Ms. Glinster will really bust them if they slug back a couple of liters of Chianti and dive naked into the Trevi Fountain at dawn. It's the parents who fall in love with the idea of enrichment and global education, not to mention getting the kid out of their hair for a week or ten days. It's the parents who communicate with other parents to receive validation that other kids are going, or reassurance that Meg's favorite buddy has signed up, or that the price seems fair—and to discuss whether Ms. Glinster really has the stuff to keep the kids off the Chianti.

While ACIS's research was not wrong—teachers are the ones who make the final choice of travel organizer—it missed the point. Yes, teachers were the ultimate clients of ACIS, but they were not the ones who contributed the most to the dialogue that made the trips happen.

When the reports starting coming in, we learned more about how the various school communities interacted and who influenced whom. We found, not surprisingly, that teachers liked to talk about the program with students, because the students would pass along the teachers' opinions to their parents. Bzz-Agent Wolfish wrote, "I am a schoolteacher in high school. I put up ACIS information on a bulletin board in my school. I reported on a trip I took to Europe through ACIS when I was a teacher in a different school a few years back. The reception was simply amazing. I have been entertaining a least five questions a day from students wanting to know more, more, and more!"

Debbiedg also weighed in. "A good friend of ours, Ken, is on the school board here and the French teacher is talking about taking a group of students to France next year. The school board was concerned about how well planned and educational the trip would really be. I talked to Ken and gave him all of the information that you guys sent me on ACIS so that he could look it over and get a feel for ACIS and what they do. I figured that these are kids from my community and I want them to have a safe, fun, and educational trip!"

The ACIS campaign demonstrated that an effective word-of-mouth program is about more than getting a message to the Perfect Target Consumer. Of equal or possibly greater value is that the campaign helps to develop a map of the communities that influence and talk with the consumer. That influence may not always directly affect the purchase decision (in this case, the students didn't really care if it was ACIS or some other trip organizer that got the job), but it plays a key role in the decision-making process.

So, who's your influencer?

It might be Jude or Johnny.

It could be Dwight from Denver.

But it's more likely to be Suprgrl379 and the kid in classroom B.

At the Barbecue

Over the next several weeks, the national campaign for SparklyPerfect continues to roll-out with superb execution by Andie and her team. The national TV and radio and print dovetail brilliantly with direct mail and couponing, in-store display, and co-op promotions. Taxi toppers are cruising America's streets.

But Andie has become preoccupied with creating a word-of-mouth campaign. She has contracted with a highly reputable local, honest word-of-mouth services provider and has spent weeks working with them. It's like nothing she's ever done before. Identifying the people who are likely to influence the PTC for SP. Sending out free samples so they can experience the product for themselves. (Three thousand of them. Ouch! But she gave away as many to Oprah, product reviewers, and PR celebs like Lizzie Grubman, so why not?) Developing a different kind of brochure to distribute to the people in the campaign. Contacting thousands of people to see if they want to take part in the campaign. Watching as, within a day, all the spots are filled.

Now, just a few days after the campaign has begun,

Andie is waiting with bated breath to hear the first reports of their activities.

To calm her nerves, she calls the WOM Pilgrim. He is backstage at the Future of Global Marketing Twenty-First–Century Conclave, just about to go on to give the keynote before five thousand people, but he is never too busy to talk with others about word-of-mouth.

"Soon you'll begin to hear what people are really thinking and saying about SparklyPerfect," he says, matter-of-factly.

"But here's what I don't get," says Andie. "Why are they doing this? They're paid nothing!"

"Because they love to talk about products—especially a product they like. They're already doing it. It's part of their social fabric. And you're giving them an opportunity to be a part of the story. It's that simple. You'll be amazed by what you learn. Just be sure to listen."

She doesn't have to wait long. That afternoon, she begins to get reports from real consumers in real situations talking about SparklyPerfect. They are revelations.

The first one she reads is from a chef at a Cuban restaurant in Miami. He writes:

"I was running late and hadn't come up with the entrée special for the night's menu. I had brought my SparklyPerfect into the restaurant kitchen and decided to see what it could do. It helped me get the meal prep done in half the time. My line cook said, 'Sparkly saved our ass.' One of the customers saw SP and wanted to know what it was."

Wait a minute, Andie thinks. Do I care if Cuban chefs are talking up SP? Where's the PTC?

She reads another one, this from a woman in Missouri:

"I bought a SparklyPerfect for a friend's daughter's wedding. She loved it. Now I'm thinking that SP is a good gift, not just for newlyweds, but for anybody setting up an apartment or home."

Andie had not really thought of SP as a gift item.

Another report completely perplexes Andie. It is from a manager at a retail outlet in Tacoma, Washington, that sells SparklyPerfect. He reports some very weird goings-on at his store:

"I notice that whenever I run a SparklyPerfect demo people buy all kinds of other stuff to go along with it. They buy small kitchen utensils like spatulas and dip spreaders. They load up on specialty condiments like hot sauces and herb rubs. They are also buying novelty garden ornaments. One guy walked out of the store with two SparklyPerfects and two topiary trolls. I said, 'What do you need two for?' He said, 'One for the main house and one for the summer place.'"

What do I make of that? Andie wonders.

The next day, SparklyPerfect catches a huge break: a SparklyPerfect taxi topper appears on a hot new episode of *CSI: Cleveland*. Andie has paid for the product placement, but SP gets far more play than she negotiated for. A suspect hops in a cab to elude the cops who are after him. Lo and behold, the cab has a SparklyPerfect topper. The cops hop in their car and give chase. The cops keep track of the suspect by following the glowing, flashing SparklyPerfect beacon. There are at least ten shots of the damn thing, including the crisp SP logo, the glam product shot, and the snappy tagline. The cops make sarcastic references to the suspect when they call in to HQ.

"We have SparklyPerfect heading west toward Beachcliff Market."

The day after the show airs, it seems as if the whole world is talking about the episode. A taxi driver writes in:

"I drive a cab in Dallas and I have a SparklyPerfect topper. Today a fare gets in and says to me, 'Step on it. The CSI guys are after me.' He laughs really loudly at his own joke. 'Funny,' I say, 'You're the fifth guy to say that.'"

The day after the CSI episode is the Sixth Annual Bardo and Megan Barbecue & Beer Block Bash, featuring SparklyPerfect.

The barbecue is a huge success. Sixty-seven people show up. There are lots of comments about SparklyPerfect. Many people don't have one, which makes Bardo very happy, because he likes showing people how it works. One guy tells Bardo that you can get an adaptor so SparklyPerfect can recharge off the car battery. "I took it camping," the guy says. "The thing is so quiet you could hear the moss growing on rocks."

Several people mention the CSI episode. One person, a marketing guy, thinks it was a very stupid product placement. "You don't want to associate your nice, friendly kitchen utensil with criminals, do you?" he says. "I'd be suing the producers right now."

The day after the barbecue, six of Bardo's guests mention SparklyPerfect to a total of thirty-eight other people. They all talk about how "the SparklyPerfect thingy" made the stuffy neighborhood meal worth going to. About how everybody was talking about the CSI episode. And, oh yes, about how Fifi (the skink) fell in the pool and had to be scooped out with the leaf catcher.

Three of Bardo's guests buy SparklyPerfects for themselves. Megan goes to the kitchen shop the next day and buys one for her dad for his sixty-fifth birthday.

Late that night, Andie is sifting through more reports. She comes across one with the subject line "WHAT'S WITH THE SQUIRREL?" It's from a young woman in New York.

"I was riding the train to work this morning thinking about taking SparklyPerfect to my parents' house with me when I visit this weekend. Suddenly, some freaky guy in a ratty squirrel suit comes running down the aisle throwing walnuts at people. I picked one up and it says SPARKLYPERFECT on it. Everybody on the train looked completely bewildered. Is this guy for real?"

Andie wonders if they should have gone with the arm-wrestling blender instead.

6

Word-of-Mouth Storytelling

Consumers talk about products all the time, but they don't talk about them in the way that marketers do. Consumers tell stories about products and services. Stories based on their own experiences and the experiences of other people.

They also tell stories about everything that surrounds the product. Including the marketing campaign. The company. What David Letterman said. Martha's opinion. How the box looked when UPS delivered it, and what happened when you opened it. Plus any other bits of material that come to mind and can be included to make the story more interesting. Positive, negative. Accurate, inaccurate. Truth or damn lies. It's all grist for the word-of-mouth story mill.

Marketers also tell stories about their products, of course. In fact, they think of themselves as masters of storytelling. Every ad is built to tell a story. Every press release tells a story. Every logo-ed nerf ball tells a story. (Sort of.) But the marketing stories are always sparklyperfect tales, in which the product looks sparkly and is perfect. Yep, the messages are consistent, the product looks, smells, feels, and tastes incredible, and it all gets summed up in a tidy, memorable catchphrase.

The consumers' stories often incorporate the marketing stories or bits of them. In fact, from the word-of-mouth study conducted by Walter J. Carl, assistant professor of communication studies at Northeastern, we learned that marketing media are a component in about 40 percent of product-related word-of-mouth. And, not surprisingly, the highest percentage of that 40 percent of media-driven interactions referenced TV—16 percent of them. Magazine ads and newspaper ads, taken together, came in a close second, mentioned in 15.4 percent of the communications (8.1 and 7.3 percent, respectively). Web banner ads got a lot of mentions, too, at 7.0 percent, followed by TV shows (5.8 percent), in-store ads (5.8 percent), and coupons (4.6 percent). All other types of marketing media—including radio spots, movie theater ads, direct mail, and Web sites—do not get mentioned much in word-of-mouth conversations.

Although media is fodder for word-of-mouth storytelling, there is often a disconnect between honest word-of-mouth stories and the marketing stories. Most people don't lean over the table at lunch and say, "Let me tell you about the features, benefits, and price/value equation of my new touch-of-Lycra summer-weight slacks." They don't refer to products by their correct names. "I really like the Gillette Mach3 Turbo Cartridges with Aloe & Vitamin E, especially in the 8-count pak." Nor do they lace their conversations with taglines: "I Let Myself Fly with Song airlines last weekend. It was like being in my living room cruising at 30,000 feet." If they're wise, they put the product into the context of their lives and experiences and needs. If they don't, they get in trouble, as BzzAgent grits29 discovered:

"My sister hosted a beautiful party at her home this afternoon.

As I prepared the dessert brew a friend of my brother-in-law walked into the kitchen. He said the coffee machine looked expensive and probably would not make any better coffee than his auto drip at home. I commented to him that the machine is just as important as the type of coffee and has a great deal to do with the overall quality of the finished brew. I then told him that the best-flavored coffee is brewed in the coffee houses using pressure, but that until recently the general public had to pay a ton of money for a machine like the coffee houses use. I told him that the Home Café is a new product that can be purchased locally and is relatively inexpensive. He started to disengage a bit at this point as he may have felt like I was selling him on something."

Hard to believe he would disengage from such an engaging story.

Now, marketers are smart. They don't expect people to be as diligent in repeating their messages as BzzAgent grits29 was, nor would they want them to be. However, when I ask clients, "What stories are people telling about your product?" I often get back blank stares. Or, they smile as if they have just been waiting for the question, drag out a PowerPoint deck the size of the Beijing phone book, and walk me through their research data on the Perfect Target Consumer, proving they know everything about the PTC including household income, what shoes they wear, their "mood" color, and their current psychographic state.

But not the stories they're telling.

Why are word-of-mouth stories so important? Because the stories are where the credibility of the product is created. Marketing stories can be delightful, clever, brilliant, charming, and hysterically funny. But, often, they aren't credible.

And that's where word-of-mouth comes in.

Jeans for the Real Bod

In 2004, we invited thousands of women to share their experiences with a new type of Lee jeans called One True Fit. Our word-of-mouth campaign was built to align with a full-scale traditional media push, which included some very well-produced and extremely sexy television commercials that featured a variety of breathtakingly beautiful women hanging around in their One True Fit jeans. The traditional media told the sparklyperfect story of One True Fit jeans. The women in the ads exuded sexiness. They were happy. And, of course, their happiness was due, in large part, to the fact that they were wearing One True Fit.

Meanwhile, across town, in the nonsparklyperfect universe, real women were trying on One True Fit at stores like JC Penney and plunking down about $30 a pair to buy them. Women liked the jeans, not because they were casting themselves as the Kate Moss ultrawaif character in the commercial, but because the jeans had been created specifically for women in their twenties and thirties. Whether they had just had a baby or their bodies were simply changing with age, these women were no longer satisfied with clothes from the juniors department but sure as hell weren't heading upstairs to the matrons department.

Of course, the women were engaged by the commercials, and so were the men. The marketer's dream was to make the product sparklyperfect for men, who could coo over the commercials, and for women, who could live the dream that the jeans would make them look and feel sexy. But the stories consumers told of them did not feature size-0 hotties in a world of late-night boogeying in blue neon clubs. No, the word-of-mouth was much more mundane than that, but a lot more credible.

As a matter of fact, a good portion of the conversations about the jeans was simply about good ol' product features and benefits. Many storylines were centered around the infamous jeans "gap," that outward pucker at the back of the jeans that can be all too revealing. (Yes, guys, women know when a bit too much of the low-low back is showing.) One of the best features of One True Fit jeans is that they do not gap. So, as women talked about the jeans, one would mention the gap factor, and then a whole conversation would ensue about how annoying gapping is. Here's the story BzzAgent sabre121 had to tell about groovin' and gappin':

"We went dancing on Saturday night with a group of friends, and the old song 'The Dip' came on and every time it was talking about 'Dipping,' I would dip down easily in my One True Fit jeans. A stranger came up to me and was asking me about my dancing ability and how I could move like that in fitted jeans. He was a guy, but I figured I could Bzz him too! I told him that these jeans were stretchy and my 'groovin' and dippin'' jeans! He laughed and he and a couple of his friends came over, and one of the girls that was with me even asked me later what the name of my jeans was! I told her and she said she would have to check them out!!"

It was amazing how many stories there were to tell about a pair of jeans. My god! They remembered how they had loved to wear Lee jeans in high school. They talked about the new, much smaller Lee jeans label, with a belt loop and little cut-copper hang-tag. They went on about the commercials and models who rolled around giggling in their jeans and about how *Marie Claire* magazine had voted One True Fit the "best jean" and *Cosmo* said One True Fit was the "best jean to fit your bod."

It was the sharing of personal experiences I would define as stories, a melange of information that blended to enable a truly shared experience. Product features, personal experiences, marketing messages, memories, and fantasies all get wrapped up into little stories that get told and retold and proliferate throughout the world of women who wear jeans.

Now, when I talk about word-of-mouth storytelling, I'm not saying that consumers are narrative geniuses who weave elaborate Aristotelian tales with gut-wrenching openings, edge-of-the-seat middles, and bust-a-vein endings. But they can be pretty amusing and engaging.

Word-of-mouth product-related stories come in a variety of genres. Sometimes they're just anecdotes, such as this one about the folks getting together after a golf game for a round of drinks, when BzzAgent jcelridge was wearing his Johnston & Murphy Lites:

"After playing golf this weekend, my golfing buddies and their wives came over to cook out last Sunday. After dinner and a few drinks their wives pulled me to the side and asked about the J&M Lites. It seems that while the guys were outside shooting the breeze around the grill, my wife had told the wives how much I liked the shoes. I don't know how the topic came up, but it seems that both my wife and I pulled 'Al Bundys' and played the part of shoe salesman."

Word-of-mouth stories are often full-fledged dramas. Here's a story from BzzAgent ChrissyJensen about Fantastik Oxy Power:

"I know I won't get points for this one but I just had to share my story and thought you would get a kick out of it! I am the preschool director at our church. This weekend being Easter, we have planned a big to-do in the children's department, decorating up the downstairs area like Jerusalem. Well, my biggest project was to borrow, rent or otherwise secure a real-live lamb for our 'barnyard' area. Yesterday I went to pick up the lamb. I had one as a child for a 4-H project, and had no memory of the really bad smell an outdoor farm animal harbors. I went to pick up this lamb in our minivan with my 4 kids. It's Colorado in March, so it was kind of muddy outside. I put this lamb into my minivan with its harness attached to the handle near the back sliding door. Needless to say, my van didn't smell so great by the time we got home. I then had the bright idea to 'wash' the lamb before taking it to church and smelling up the place. I put the lamb into the bathtub. All the kids watched, laughing. He is a very calm lamb and didn't make a fuss, but I had a HUGE mess to clean up. I mean BIG. So, being a dedicated BzzAgent, I got out the Fantastik [Oxy Power].

"It cleaned the bathtub really really well—also the floor and the splatter marks on the walls from where the lamb did the dog-shake maneuver to get the water off. Then I attacked the car. I had put a blanket down, but evidently did not take into consideration any wet type of excrement the lamb might produce. After tossing the blanket into the trash, I used the Fantastik to get the ick out of the carpets, the lamb slobber off the sliding door, and the muddy footprints off the door steps. Whew!!! I went through 1½ rolls of paper towels and a whole bottle of the Oxy, but MAN was it worth it! My hubby came home last night and thanked me for keeping the lamb out of the house! I am very thankful that the product worked consistently well on the huge mess like it always does on smaller messes in the house!

"I guess I did Bzz a couple of people about it. I told my friends at church about the ordeal and how well the product worked (everything I said above) and my friend who has a horse farm said she would have to get some if it worked that well on farm smells! She totally took my word on it and will probably be out buying a bottle today (since I talked her into taking the lamb home in HER car last night to stay at her house in an empty stall in her horse barn!)."

Stories can also be tragicomic, like this one from BzzAgent karnj about Anheuser World Lager beer (previously known as Anheuser World Select or AWS):

"This weekend we buried my grandfather ... a sweet Irishman. He would have enjoyed the AWS unstoppably! After the funeral, my husband, brother, and his wife decided to have lunch at a pub nearby. I bought the first round ... deliberately. 'We'll have 4 AWS, please.' I say. My brother, being a much more knowledgeable beer drinker than I, looks at me puzzled. He'd obviously not heard of it and immediately jumps into the 'How dare you order me skunk water!' WELL! I watched his reaction carefully. Very intrigued, he was. The embossed bottle is a NICE touch ... sucked him in right away. We toasted Pop, and the look on my brother's face when he drank first was priceless. His eyebrows rose, then he started reading the label. 'Who makes this??' Mind you, my late father was a Budweiser freak, and my brother inherited that, so he knows beer. His wife can drink him under the table, so she kept up well. Al bought the next two rounds ... all AWS. I think I've snagged him. And his wife. Not to mention my OWN husband, but he doesn't count. He'd drink anything I put in front of him. So thanks to my Pop—God rest his soul—I think you've got another consumer."

The stories may be more thought-provoking, rather like an existential mininovel with lots of soul searching, not much action, and a downer ending. BzzAgent JAWIEMANN was involved in the campaign for Tom Peters's book *Project04: Snapshots of Excellence in Unstable Times*.

"In the life of a recent college graduate, the questions and tremors that constantly attack the mind and soul seem to return to the question, 'What now?' My friends and I, all 22 or 23, clearly have no idea. While some have jobs and others are on blindly-chosen career paths, we're all still convinced that we're confused and unsure whether to stray from the safe course of white collar jobs or to find/fabricate some type of passion. On this particular afternoon, I was sitting with a couple of my friends at a local diner on the Upper West Side, having a late brunch and talking about the new year—our contrived hopes and fears and overall uncertainty, as all of us hated our jobs at the moment, despite their vast differences: teacher, music agent, consultant, secretary. After much discussion about how much everybody hated their jobs, I said, 'There have got to be people who actually enjoy their jobs, right? Right? I mean, I've been reading this thing by Tom Peters, *Project04: Snapshots of Excellence in Unstable Times*, which lists all these amazing people with passions that really change the way business works, like the Apple guy and Lucas and guys like that.' My friend Dan said, 'It makes sense, I guess. Just hard to do.' I said, 'I think that's just the comfort zone thing. This guy Tom Peters is all about getting yourself out of it.'"

And, yes, word-of-mouth stories can sometimes unfold as an action comedy. Here's a story from BzzAgent Sweetnlow, who participated in the campaign for the fragrance from Ralph Lauren called Ralph Cool:

"Today wasn't my ordinary Friday. Normally I would have to stay home and watch my kid sister, who is ten years old. But today, my brother didn't go to work. So my boyfriend and I went to our friend Jeremy's body shop. When we got there it was just us three (Jeremy, Gary—he's my boyfriend—and me) plus his mom, dad, and cousin Cindy. Jeremy, Gary and I were talking about cars and such when suddenly Cindy got mad because it was so hot and she was starting to smell like sweat. I handed her my bottle of RL Cool perfume. She looked at me in amazement. I told her to spray it and she wouldn't smell so bad. So she did just that. A spritz on her head, chest, neck, butt, knees, and her feet, then one in the air and she walked into it. Then another in the air and backed into it. Of course there was a strong sense of this fragrance in the air and all of the girls that were there came rushing over. They were all talking about it and spraying more. I had to fight them to get it back."

Yikes. I doubt that any marketers could have imagined that one. But the product still comes out as the star of the story.

Every company should know the stories its consumers are sharing. Whether it's a bunch of kids getting the munchies and eating your cereal or a room full of executives gabbing about a new business theory from the guru's book, stories are the most important component of word-of-mouth dialogue.

The Romance of the Bugaboo

Word-of-mouth stories also end up as fantasies or romances, especially when they're told before the consumer actually experiences the product.

For example, when we were expecting our first child, my wife spent a lot of time thinking about what kind of stroller to buy. She decided that there was only one carriage to have, the Bugaboo Frog. It's a high-riding European job that looks like a cross between a shopping cart and an off-road vehicle for babies.

What made her decide that the Bugaboo was THE stroller? She took all the info she had gathered up about all the various strollers available and plugged it into all the other info and ideas she had about our lives and came up with stories that brought the two together.

There is a guy who lives down the street from us who never shovels the $&*$#! snow in front of his house. That makes for very tricky maneuvering, even for a normal, reasonably able-bodied person. So, my wife starts picturing herself pushing the baby stroller along the sidewalk, until she reaches the moonlike surface in front of his house. Does she manhandle the stroller up and over it? Or does she squeeze between the cars and push along the street? With Bugaboo, problem solved. It has two little front wheels that rotate completely to facilitate tight turns. It has two big wheels with all-terrain tires whose treads will gain traction in the snow. In short, walking home with the kid becomes a good story to tell rather than a nightmare.

One story leads to another. The creators of the Bugaboo are Dutch. My wife and I love the Netherlands. We got engaged there. We hope to live there someday. One of the founders of Bugaboo is an artist. Design is very important to me. My wife has, in the past, been responsible for the design flow of Web sites. Pretty soon we were telling ourselves all kinds of baby and stroller stories. We talked about the fact that the designers were Dutch, then had a conversation about the weird cat museum we once walked into accidentally on Prinsengracht. My wife thought she had seen a Bugaboo in the corner, with two cats nestled in the baby basket. Yes, strangely, this made us feel good about the Bugaboo. If it was OK for the museum-cat-people, in our favorite country on the planet, then why not for us?

Our Bugaboo story was—no question—a romance. We had no direct experience with the product. We were simply borrowing the marketing messages, the sparklyperfect version of the stroller, throwing in all the other indirect stuff we could (literature, Web site visits, stories from people we knew), plus all our own thoughts and experiences, and putting ourselves into the new story as the happy heroes. And, of course, we were validating each other's opinions.

We have seen just how powerful the sparklyperfect story can be many, many times in our BzzAgent campaigns. People get very excited about a new product when they first learn about it—but BEFORE they've actually touched it or used it—and they can't wait to tell others about it. They want to start telling stories right away.

This one is from BzzAgent Mike24, who had just been accepted to participate in a campaign for Castrol SYNTEC oil.

"As soon as I the joined Castrol SYNTEC oil campaign, I was

excited about telling someone about it. I signed on to Instant Messaging and I saw that my friend, Chris, was on. I asked him if he usually changed his own oil. He responded, 'I always change my oil. That's because my dad took his truck to a mechanic once for an oil change. The oil they used actually damaged his engine. They had to take the stuff off the market.' I told Chris, 'Then you really should try this new synthetic oil called Castrol SYNTEC. It looks pretty good. I'm getting some in the mail soon, but I think it's available at Auto Zone.' He said, 'I always use synthetic oil. I'll give it a try.'"

OK, so Mike24 wasn't as gaga about Castrol as my wife was about Bugaboo, but he was relatively revved up when you consider he was talking about a can of refined petroleum. The promise of SYNTEC gained a lot of credibility for both Mike24 and Chris, with the story of how horribly things can go wrong when you get stuck with an inferior oil, as Chris's poor dad had. The sparklyperfect version of SYNTEC sounds good. The word-of-mouth version makes it sound like a godsend.

Connecting and Disconnecting

When the marketing story and the word-of-mouth stories align, it can be word-of-mouth nirvana.

Think about UPS, for example. In 2002, UPS began a marketing campaign that told the company's story in a new way. It was all about what Brown "can do for you" and it centered on the UPS delivery guy. The sparklyperfect version of the man in the brown suit was a hunky, charming guy who lit up every office he walked into and had the answer to every business problem every customer had.

OK, we all know the reality of UPS drivers is not quite that. But UPS got it. They had based their marketing story on what people really talked about in offices around the world: the guy who shows up at your office or home. The word-of-mouth stories are all about who the guy is, what he looks like, how he delivers the package. In our office, we're still talking about the time our upright, nice-guy UPS driver hit on one of the young women. That's not exactly what she had in mind when she thought about what Brown could do for her. We also talk about the awesome guy with twenty tattoos who would come back three times a day and just hang out. (Yes, UPS, he got all his deliveries done on time, and we probably did spend more because of him, so chill.) Or the guy who replaced him, who had only three teeth.

We talked about the real UPS guys and we saw the fantasy UPS guys in the ads. The versions looked very different. But the heart of the story was the same. And that made for very positive word-of-mouth for UPS.

The consumer stories about Netflix also line up well with the marketing messages. People love to talk about how it's much smarter to use Netflix than to rent movies from the local video store. You don't have to schlep out when you're tired and twist your neck sideways to look at the titles of a bunch of second-rate movies you don't know anything about. You can keep the movies as long as you want, so you don't discover that you could have purchased four movies with the amount of money you blew on that movie that dropped behind the couch and you didn't return for two weeks. You tell the story of your life as a smart Netflix user. Everything about Netflix lends itself to a story you can tell, from how you watch more and better movies now (and drop the name of some forgotten French masterpiece like *Pickpocket*) to how you have fewer fights with your partner about what to rent. The facts are necessary for good storytelling, but it's the personalization that makes it into something that is worth creating word-of-mouth about.

A little disconnect between the sparklyperfect marketing story and the real consumer word-of-mouth stories is to be expected. But sometimes the marketing story is so far off that the consumer really can't bridge the gap.

Consider the Segway Human Transporter (HT). Some years ago, the inventor Dean Kamen announced that he had developed a product that would change the world. At first, he did not say exactly what the product was. He didn't even say what it would be called. He referred to the new product only as "it." His coyness drove people to talk about what the new, new thing might be. For the better part of a year, everyone was talking about "it" even though they didn't even know what it really was.

At last, with the buzz going crazy planetwide, Kamen unveiled his fantastic new invention. It turned out that the Segway HT was a motorized, two-wheeled, scooterlike vehicle designed to whisk a single person from place to place more quickly than he could walk, but without the physical effort required to pedal a bike. The best part about it was that it was so perfectly balanced that anybody could ride it without much training and with no danger of falling off.

The marketing messages for Segway promised a whole new era of transportation. Whole cities would be redesigned around the Segway. It would alleviate air pollution. It would enable handicapped, out-of-shape, or immobilized people to gain new freedom of movement. Seniors would never leave home without it. It would revolutionize all kinds of jobs. Mail carriers and parking meter attendants, people with short commutes to work, employees in giant warehouses and theme parks—people everywhere—would leave old-fashioned walking behind and start Segwaying instead. The number of cars would plummet along with the pollution they create. The planet, in short, would be transformed.

While the prelaunch hype was going on, people told stories

about the hype and shared their opinions about how the Segway might change the world. They made up stories about Dean Kamen. They talked about the unbelievable press coverage.

Then the product was launched. A few people started buying them. The city of Atlanta outfitted a few of its Information Guides with them. Almost immediately, the word-of-mouth stories did not even remotely connect to the marketing story. They sliced into the credibility of the marketing claims. People said that tourists were having a lot of fun pushing the Info Guides off their scooters. Then President Bush (forty-three, not forty-one) took a test ride on a Segway and fell off. But the marketing story was that it was impossible to fall off! Next, the city of San Francisco banned people from riding a Segway on its sidewalks. It just got worse and worse. The word-of-mouth Segway stories were horror flicks and sitcoms.

What Stories Tell

When marketers listen to word-of-mouth stories, they often learn things about the product—about its features or how it is used or who likes it—that can be very useful in refining the message, defining the Perfect Target Consumer, or even improving the product itself.

We ran a campaign for Kellogg's Smorz, a sweet breakfast cereal aimed at kids. ("What's more FUN than a crunchy GRAHAM cereal wrapped in rich CHOCOLATEY COATING with MARSHMALLOWS!") While the Smorz folks intended this to be a breakfast cereal only for kids, we got a lot of reports about people who were not kids who ate Smorz at different times or in unexpected places. We learned that Smorz was seen as a snack food of choice for thirty-somethings because it provided quick energy when they were hiking or sporting. Here's how BzzAgent starlettbebe told the story:

"My family and friends were planning to go hiking in the mountains just to spend a day outside together, enjoy the scene and each other's company. We usually take the standard hiking snacks—chocolate and crackers and plenty of water. This time I decided to make a Smorz trail mix. A lot of Smorz cereal, some peanuts, fresh cashews, assorted M&Ms, and dried berries (raisins, cranberries, etc.) to put some pizzazz in our escapade. A few hours into the hike, most of us were hungry and exhausted. When the chocolate and cracker supply was exhausted, I pulled out the giant bag of trail mix I had made. Everyone was grateful for this pleasant little surprise, especially our friends. They don't have kids around the house anymore, they're all off at college, so they don't keep up with the new foods that come out. They absolutely loved the Smorz! Even though they're older and more sophisticated, they still have enough youth left in them to get addicted to this chocolatey cereal. I'm pretty sure they'll be heading over to buy some Smorz for their house!"

Kellogg's had not thought about Smorz as the hero in a story about senior hikers. Nor had it considered many other, even more unlikely, stories that the cereal might figure in. For example, we got several reports from twenty-somethings who told us that Smorz is a truly delightful treat, especially when you have a case of the munchies. BzzAgent starlettbebe described how Smorz rescued him from having to eat hideous food at a leadership conference he attended with a bunch of teenagers:

"I went on a leadership conference with a bunch of other teenage youths. It was an opportunity to meet new people, learn new skills, socialize, and develop ourselves. I was looking forward to every bit of this trip—except for the dreaded food. It was like a sleep-away camp, and we all know how sleep-away camps are with their food. It seems that no matter how hard they try, cafeteria food just doesn't cut it. I've had experiences with food poisoning from camp food, so I decided to bring some of my own along. When breakfast rolled around, I whipped out my trusty box of Smorz. While everyone was stuck eating 'eggs' and dried-up bacon, I had my nice comfort food of Smorz. And of course, everyone looked over to see what I was eating. I told them it was Smorz, a new cereal from Kellogg's. I passed the box around (out of pity for them having to eat camp food) and everyone had a bit to eat. The general response to Smorz was genuine interest. They liked it, but I'm not sure how many are going to run out and get their own box. Although I may not have converted anyone into a Smorz fanatic, I did make some new friends and we did definitely enjoy a nice breakfast that morning."

There is little doubt that when BzzAgent starlettbebe talks about his camp days, Smorz will be a featured story.

Stories also serve as our way to connect with each other about how involved we are with a product, as a way to validate our opinions and our experiences. Patagonia is a company that knows this well. According to Craig Wilson, director Global eMedia, people are constantly telling him stories about their experiences with Patagonia products. They can't help themselves. Craig knows that as soon as they learn that he works for Patagonia, he's going to hear a hiking or skiing or swimming or biking story that features a Patagonia jacket or socks or piece of gear.

So, naturally, almost as soon as I picked up the phone to talk with him, I had to tell Craig my own story about the Patagonia jacket I got in college and am still wearing ten years later. My wife thinks that the jacket is starting to look pretty tired. But not a single thing on it has failed. Not a thread is out of place. The zipper is flawless. It still keeps me warm. Here I am, a guy who helps companies integrate word-of-mouth into their marketing efforts. I'm ridiculously aware of every dialogue I have about a product or service. And I find myself blabbering out the story of my ten-year-old Patagonia fleece and how my wife wants me to chuck it and how miraculous it is that the thing still keeps me warm.

Why do people feel so compelled to tell Craig their stories? It's because Patagonia has built its brand on word-of-mouth stories. In fact, it never really told a sparklyperfect marketing story at all. Its primary marketing effort is a straightforward, here's-the-merchandise direct mail catalog. So there can be no disconnect between the sparklyperfect version and the word-of-mouth version. Patagonia has always listened to what its customers are saying about how they use the products, and it has kept on creating and selling products that fit with those stories. As a result, Patagonia is one of those companies with incredibly high brand loyalty and a very strong reputation for genuineness and honesty.

Marketing is storytelling. Word-of-mouth is storytelling, too, but it has the credibility of a real opinion based on real perceptions and experiences. Consumers are listening very carefully to the marketing story and retell it as they please. The best marketing stories are the ones that are based on how the product or service actually looks in real life (like the UPS Brown campaign) but still allow plenty of room for the consumer's imagination to go wild (like with Bugaboo).

I'm thinking of buying a new car. What story do you want to tell me?

A Pimple on SparklyPerfect

It's two months after launch. Andie's team is getting ready to breathe a sigh of relief. Not only are the campaign elements working well, sales are starting to exceed plan. Farman has been witnessed meeting with the CEO in the GlobalGajitz cafeteria, talking about SparklyPerfect sales data and reading word-of-mouth reports. Both men were chortling.

Then, WISCONSIN happens.

Andie hears about it first in a word-of-mouth report from a young woman in Wisconsin:

"I like my SparklyPerfect so much that I decided to get some new accessories for it, including the pasta feature. One night, my boyfriend was coming over with some friends and I decided to use the pasta accessory to make dinner because we all love fettuccine. I got everything ready and then switched on SP and, crack!, the pasta thing broke. Needless to say, no fettuccine for us that night. Next day, I took my SP back to the store where I bought it. They told me I had at-tached the pasta part wrong, so that I wasn't eligible for a free replacement. I said I'd buy a new one but they didn't have one in stock. Will someone please tell GlobalGajitz that they have a problem with the pasta feature?"

Andie remembers another report about the pasta feature, so she immediately gets together with the product people. Turns out the pasta accessory has been redesigned and sourced from a new supplier. The new version can be incorrectly fitted into the old machine and can break in use. However, the part works fine when properly assembled, which most people manage to do.

"You'd have to be an idiot to assemble it incorrectly," says the guy from design.

Andie and her team debate the issue. They find a total of just two word-of-mouth reports on the "pasta problem," as they call it. They play with the product. The designer is right: you have to really work at it to put the new part on the old machine incorrectly. They check the original focus group data. No one had ever put the two pieces together in the "wrong" way or even tried to. Maybe these are very isolated cases. Maybe they should just do nothing and the problem will go away of its own accord.

But Andie's Technorati and Feedster accounts keep finding new blog mentions of the pasta problem and other customer comments. And, soon enough (too soon), the SparklyPerfect pasta problem becomes a hot topic. One subject line reads "SPARKLYPERFECT IS ANYTHING BUT." Not only has the writer had the pasta part break, but she was so startled when it happened that she dropped SP on her foot. "So now I have a broken machine and a broken toe," she writes. "Does anybody know a good personal injury lawyer?"

Then a blog media blowhard, one Sanjay Cicalanac,

jumps into the fray, blowing the issue out of proportion just to stimulate controversy. Soon rumors are circulating that SP is a danger. That GlobalGajitz knew about the problem all along. That there's a huge cover-up. Not only that, the company outsources all its manufacturing to a country with the worst human rights record on the planet.

The rumors breed other rumors and soon the Web seems to be awash with gleefully determined detractors, making fun of SparklyPerfect and calling for it to be removed from the market.

Andie is in a sweat. All their perfectly timed and beautifully integrated marketing efforts are in danger of being scuttled! Tossing and turning, unable to sleep, she puts in a call to the WOM Pilgrim, even though it's 3 A.M. in Abu Dhabi, where the Pilgrim is preparing a pitch to Kofi Annan and the United Nation's newly formed marketing unit.

"What do you think we should do?" she asks him.

"The negative people are very loud," says the Pilgrim. "But you have more supporters than you think. And, now, Kofi awaits."

That day, Andie's team runs a quick poll of all the participants in their word-of-mouth campaign to get their opinions on what they should do. After considering their responses, Andie decides to go completely public and come clean. They post an explanation of the pasta accessory problem on the front page of the Web site. They offer to replace the pasta accessory for anybody with the original machine. They also post detailed instructions on how to attach the pasta accessory and offer a 20 percent–off promotion on summer color snap-on sleeves.

Meanwhile, Bardo runs into Cam in the produce department at the supermarket. "Hey, Bardo, have you heard about the SparklyPerfect scam?" Cam asks.

"What are you talking about?" Bardo asks.

"There's some safety issue and they're doing a phony recall or something."

"Safety issue? How do you know?"

"I read it online. I'm disgusted. 'Beyond Awesome.' Yeah, RIGHT!"

Bardo, to his surprise, feels his blood start to rise. He has never had a safety issue with SparklyPerfect. In fact, it is so well made and easy to use that Megan lets Lily and her friends cook with it in the kitchen (with adult supervision, of course).

That night, Bardo goes online and finds the debate raging about SparklyPerfect. He suddenly feels a sense of loyalty to the product, a loyalty he didn't even know he had. He adds a comment to a long string on one of the sites:

"NEVER HAD A PROBLEM WITH THIS GREAT PRODUCT!" Bardo writes. "My wife and I use our SP all the time. We use it to prepare pasta meals at least once a week. SparklyPerfect was the hit of our annual barbecue this year. My 7-year-old daughter can put on the pasta accessory all by herself. I think some people should get a life."

Andie sees Bardo's post and silently thanks him. Not two hours later, when she checks again, there is another post on the same site, from another SparklyPerfect supporter, who says, "When I heard about this whole brouhaha, I tried to put the pasta accessory on wrong and couldn't do it. Maybe somebody had a little too much wine while they were cooking dinner?"

Within a couple of days, the tide has turned. Andie is amazed to see that the blogs are filled with posts defending SparklyPerfect. When the replacement offer and color sleeve promotion hits, there is a noticeable spike in sales.

Eventually, the detractors shut up—and the world goes back to using their SPs to cook fettuccine.

7

The Weird Value
of Negativity

It's a fundamental rule of marketing that the messages about a product or service must always be 100 percent positive—sparklyperfect. But, in the world of word-of-mouth, negativity can have wonderfully weird and even dramatically positive effects.

Negative word-of-mouth is what adds credibility to a product. Everybody knows that few products are 100 percent perfect, nor do they expect them to be. As much as consumers would like to believe in the marketing fantasy, they seek out word-of-mouth to find out the truths. They want to know what they get when they buy. They want to be sure they know where the faults lie. The power of word-of-mouth for the consumer is that it helps us make a more informed decision.

Negative word-of-mouth is also an invaluable source of feedback for the product, brand, and company. It is very possible to run focus groups, do test marketing and in-home consumer interviews, and still not discover how consumers are going to communicate about the product as they use it and integrate it into their lives. But, there is a huge amount of information available in the conversations of individuals who experience the product every day. The answers to the age-old marketing questions are in the people who are walking the streets of your small city or large urban sprawl. Why search for the needle of an answer in the haystack of a tiny room with a one-way mirror and a dish of Mars bars for those who answer the questions most effectively? Negative feedback should always be listened to with great attention and shared throughout a company. Seeking it out should be paramount.

The way a company responds to negative word-of-mouth can create positive word-of-mouth. According to a study by W. Glynn Mangold et al., half of all negative word-of-mouth comes from consumers who feel a sense of injustice about the way they are treated by a company when they have a problem, rather than by the shortcomings in the product or service itself. So, the way a company responds to negative word-of-mouth becomes an important part of the conversation, possibly the most important part of it. In fact, I'd say that companies with mediocre products and amazing customer service have less negative word-of-mouth than companies with great products and crummy customer service.

Finally, when negative word-of-mouth gets particularly noisy and nasty, it often creates a backlash of positivity. People who like the product but aren't particularly inclined to talk much about it often become vocal when they think a product is being unfairly slammed. We call these people the quiet advocates, and there are often many more of them for a product than there are passionate evangelists.

When they start to speak up, they can move mountains.

Apple Fixes Its Dirty Little Secret

Although the Apple iPod took the market by storm, due in part to copious amounts of word-of-mouth from Apple evangelists, not all of the word-of-mouth was positive.

One customer, a New York–based multimedia artist and filmmaker named Casey Neistat, bought an iPod in early 2002. He loved it. He listened to it as he rode his bike to his TriBeCa studio. But, after about eighteen months, the battery started to lose its oomph, wouldn't hold a charge, and finally croaked. This annoyed Mr. Neistat, a Mac loyalist. According to his Web site, ipodsdirtysecret.com, he took his ailing iPod to the stunning Apple store on Prince Street in Manhattan for repair. He was told that there was no replacement battery available and that his only option was to buy a whole new unit.

At that point, Neistat was getting steamed. He called Apple's toll-free customer service line and heard the same story. So he wrote on his Web site, "I then sent my iPod to the Apple Executive office, addressed to Steve Jobs, with a note explaining my situation and requesting a replacement battery. The Apple Executive office contacted me via telephone to explain that Apple does not repair or replace dead iPod batteries and that it was policy of the company to recommend to the customer to purchase a new iPod when the battery fails. I then looked into it and purchased a third party replacement battery, which was not endorsed by Apple. After the complicated installation, my iPod did not work at all, even when plugged in."

So far, so bad. Unlike most consumers, who would simply moan about the lousy battery and possibly badmouth Apple for two or three months, Casey and his brother Van decided to make a film about the experience and post it on the Internet. Their movie, called *iPod's Dirty Secret,* showed a young man (presumably one of the Neistat brothers) spray painting the words IPOD'S UNREPLACEABLE BATTERY LASTS ONLY 13 MONTHS on iPod billboards at various places around New York.

Millions of people visited the site. Thousands downloaded the movie and sent it along to the millions of people in their networks. Soon people around the world were talking about the film and the battery issue and the Neistat brothers and Apple. "We got close to one thousand emails the first couple of days," Casey Neistat told a *Washington Post* reporter. "Eighty percent of our mail was positive, saying they liked the sardonically irreverent way we did it. But there were die-hard Mac fans who were mad at us, who were panicking because they feel like we might cause somebody to not buy a Macintosh."

All of this could have dealt a crushing blow to Apple's extremely hot new product. A short-lived battery could well have put a serious dent in sales. There were, after all, other MP3 players available on the market. Everyone was watching to see how Apple would respond. Would the iPod survive? How would Jobs explain this one?

Apple handled the negative word-of-mouth just as it should have. First, it listened. Then, within days, the company not only fixed the battery problem, it changed its service policy. It began to offer a replacement battery for $99 and an extended warranty for $59. And, as word-of-mouth has it, Apple sent Casey Neistat a brand new iPod.

Not only did this please a lot of customers, it satisfied the Neistat brothers. They posted a message on their ipodsdirtysecret site. "We acknowledge Apple's new battery replacement policy," they wrote. "Our movie is a documentation of our experience." OK, not a glowing endorsement, but at least recognition that they had been listened to and the problem had been resolved.

Apple turned around a potentially ugly situation by listening to the negative feedback about the battery and responding to it quickly and effectively. Remember that the real beef the Neistats had with Apple was not so much that the battery went kaput—everybody accepts that batteries do not last forever— but that its customer service was so inflexible and unaccommodating. It was the customer service rep at the store and the exasperating helpline—along with the lack of a replacement battery—that drove the negative word-of-mouth. Once Apple responded, the negative word-of-mouth dropped. Instantly. And its detractors were now its advocates.

Academics who have studied the word-of-mouth phenomenon confirm that the iPod story is hardly unique. Marsha Richins, Myron Watkins Distinguished Professor and professor of marketing at the University of Missouri, did a study that shows that a person's tendency to engage in negative word-of-mouth is positively related to the level of dissatisfaction the person feels. In other words, people are more likely to make negative comments the more dissatisfied they feel with a product or service. Not too surprising.

Further, Professor Richins found that consumers' tendency to go negative is cranked up by their perception of how the company responds to the complaint. If the consumer thinks that the company isn't listening, they are more likely to go ballistic. Richins also learned that a customer is particularly apt to get negative when they blame the company for their dissatisfaction. If a customer doesn't like the product but there's nothing particularly wrong with it, they may not say anything negative about it. But if they think they've been duped or betrayed or misled, they will.

These findings are consistent with those of Jeffrey G. Blodgett of the University of Mississippi. He and his colleagues found that consumers' tendency to engage in negative word-of-mouth is largely dependent on their perception of the complaint process. That is, consumers are less likely to engage in negative word-of-mouth if they feel that they can connect with the company, are being heard, are well treated during the process, and that the outcome is fair. The implication is that a company can overcome a great deal of negative reaction to a product or brand if it has a good process in place for listening and responding and takes positive action to fix its faults, just as Apple did with the iPod.

Often, by taking good care of customers, a company will create advocates—people who become passionate about the company almost completely because of the way they've been treated. The interaction that the customer has with the company becomes part of the word-of-mouth about the product. In fact, it can be the most important story the consumer tells.

Negativity Is Part of the Brew

We saw the strange morphology of negativity very clearly in a campaign we conducted in 2004 for the Home Café, a single-serving coffee-brewing machine. The machine is compact and meant for use at home or the office. The coffee grounds are contained in single serving "pods"—little packages of coffee, almost like tea bags—that are made by Folgers and are available in various flavors. The obvious benefit of the machine is that it enables the user to make just one cup of coffee, with many flavors to choose from.

Although there were a number of single-serving café units coming onto the market at about the same time, Home Café had a good head start. It had the considerable appeal of the Folgers brand name associated with the product, and the machine was manufactured by Black & Decker, the respected maker of tools and appliances.

Home Café decided to work with BzzAgent to create a word-of-mouth campaign, as just one part of a large and well-planned marketing effort that would include television and print advertising and direct mail. It was also planning to do some alternative marketing, such as product placements. The product would have, in fact, a cameo role on *Survivor*. The Home Café would be given as a reward to the winners of one of the challenges in the jungle. After weeks of chewing sugar cane as a stimulant, they would get to share with each other the delights of fresh-brewed flavored coffee. The word-of-mouth from these marketing activities was intended to boost credibility in conjunction with the awareness-building effects of the advertising and promotions.

Before BzzAgent takes on any campaign, we review samples of the product to help us understand whether it will fit well with our community. This is not about deciding whether to endorse or recommend the product. That we do not do. We are not Underwriter's Laboratory or *Consumer Reports*. We simply want to determine if our community would likely be interested in considering and talking about the product. We sometimes decline to take on a campaign for a product because we believe it would not arouse any interest in our community. We said no to a cigarette company, for example—even though it was for a campaign aimed at only its existing customers—because the company didn't want us to work on an antismoking campaign at the same time. But, although we're not an underwriter, we are very concerned about the quality and integrity of the products we work with. In fact, we get pretty excited about testing and evaluating.

So, the arrival of our Home Café samples caused quite a hubbub at the office. A few folks tore open the box and immediately got busy setting up the machine. Instructions were passed back and forth. Someone went to get water. Boxes of coffee pods were opened and the pods were sniffed. Mugs were grabbed off the kitchen shelves.

With the machine all ready to go, we poured in the water, selected a Classic Roast pod, and pushed the button. The machine whirred and vibrated. We stood around like eager kids, and watched the machine drip out its single serving of coffee. The aroma was quite bold. We elected one of the staff to be the first taster. She smelled. She sipped. She swallowed. She wrinkled her nose. "Tastes like plastic," she said. We passed the mug around. Most folks agreed. The taste wasn't what they were expecting. We decided to brew up another mug, this time with a French-Vanilla pod. While we were waiting for it to brew, someone looked at the instructions again. "It says it will take a few brewings for the plasticy taste to go away," he read. "Ah-hahhhh!" we all said. We brewed several more cups and still no one was doing backflips over the taste. One of our engineers really liked the French Vanilla flavor, but the overall marks for the coffee taste weren't high.

After the tasting, we decided to set aside our personal reactions to the flavor of the coffee and think about the product in relation to the Home Café target consumer and the BzzAgent community. We didn't fit the criteria of the target consumer at all. We were not single-cup drinkers. We had access to coffee shops up and down the street. We weren't concerned about brewing up a pot with no one else around to polish it off.

So, we did some research and learned that there is a huge audience of home brewers out there. There are people all over the country who don't have a coffee house on every corner. There are loads of people who don't have the time to run downtown every time they want to grab themselves a caffeine jolt. It seemed that there were plenty of people who would value a single-cup home-brewing system. We also found plenty of people who said that they like the taste of the Home Café brew. So we decided that our evaluation of this product wasn't consistent with the target audience, and there were lots of people in our community who fit the Home Café profile. We decided we could help.

However, our research also uncovered some reviews of other aspects of the performance of the Home Café machine. Some reviewers thought that it was an amazing little gadget and well worth purchasing. Others said that the machine was noisy. That it didn't get the water hot enough, that it didn't fill the cup or else overfilled it. We found this a little worrisome. We knew that a word-of-mouth campaign wouldn't be able to add value if the machine didn't work properly.

But we thought Home Café was an interesting product and could capture a lot of word-of-mouth attention. Just the idea of a single-serve home-brew system was enough to stimulate word-of-mouth. A lot of word-of-mouth, after all, is about what could be, about the anticipation of trying a new thing. It's about the promise of the idea. The fact that we had encountered a few negatives didn't dampen our enthusiasm for the idea of Home Café and our desire to talk about it.

So, Tim Lash, our account director for Home Café, picked up the phone and we got on a call with our client. He was not particularly concerned with our reactions to the taste of the coffee, because taste is such an individual thing. Besides, Home Café's tests had shown that its target audience was satisfied with the taste. He was concerned, however, with the reports we had found about the performance issues. He told us that there had been a few kinks in the early production runs and that some of those machines were not performing up to specifications, particularly concerning the temperature of the water. But the problems had been fixed and the latest batch of machines was working well. He guessed that we might have been sent machines from an early run. The water temperature had been fine with our machine, but our client said that he would send us the latest version anyway, so we could conduct another coffee-guzzling field test.

We received the new machines a few days later. They looked the same as the ones we had received earlier. We field-tested again. No water temp issues. No water volume issues. No changes in the taste of the coffee, either. We were good to go. We gave the green light, and looked forward to another successful campaign without the slightest inkling of the problems we were about to encounter.

We launched the Home Café BzzCampaign in the fall of 2004. We had three thousand slots for agents and offered the campaign to about ten thousand members of the community. It took only thirty-six hours for the campaign to fill up—a good sign. It can take much longer for some campaigns to fill all its slots. Almost immediately after the campaign was closed, we starting receiving requests from other agents who had not responded in time and wanted to get in. BzzAgent Supermomm81 wrote,

"Hi, I was just wondering if I could request an invite to this campaign. I love coffee and I have many friends and family that I could see myself promoting this to. I get together with my in-laws every weekend and we sit around and drink coffee. I go for coffee with my friends once a week to chat. I have wonderful opportunities to get out word-of-mouth. I understand if you can't do this, but I was just wondering. I really would like the chance to be a part of this campaign. Thank you very much."

Sorry, Supermomm81. We wish we had had a slot for you. But we already had our three thousand agents ready to go. Many were a good match with the Home Café target audience profile. It was clear that they were interested and wanted to get involved and couldn't wait to start drinking coffee and talking about the machine.

We started receiving an avalanche of reports from agents as soon as they had been accepted into the campaign. The vast majority of them were incredibly excited about being part of the campaign and they said that they couldn't wait to receive their Home Café in the mail. Many of them started Bzzing the product right away.

BzzAgent sweetshaye wrote, "I haven't received my Home Café box yet but I had a wonderful opportunity last night to create some Bzz so I jumped on it! My father-in-law called to verify his plans for Christmas. He always comes to our house for the holidays so he wanted to make sure everything was set. Last year our coffee machine was broken and that took him over the edge so he was joking around with me about it last night and he wanted to know if he needed to bring his own machine!!! I said I was actually getting a new machine that was awesome and then I told him about Home Café. I told him that he would be able to brew his own special flavor and that we wouldn't have to have a big pot of one flavor. He was excited about being able to make his own cup cuz he likes to be different and difficult (I just threw that in myself). So I told him he could check out the Web site but, quite frankly, since he is so excited about it, I might just go get him one for under the tree! He is actually going to go pick up some pods and bring them for Christmas day! So I am hoping we get the machine in time :)"

All over the country, agents were Bzzing the Home Café like mad. BzzAgent Hj033 Bzzed the other women in her office. "I know how much our office needs coffee," she wrote, "and how TERRIBLE our coffee is here." BzzAgent dipiazza was shopping in a Target when she Bzzed a gentleman who was looking for two coffee machines to buy as gifts. BzzAgent tmnewmark told her brother about Home Café over the phone. "Since he lives alone, I thought it would be perfect for him," she wrote. "He told me, 'It sounds interesting, but I've decided to cut down on coffee.' Oh well, at least I tried."

Soon enough, people started receiving their packages containing the Home Café units and began to experience the product for themselves. Their ecstatic reports told stories of people brewing up single serves of coffee for their spouses, parents, co-workers, and UPS drivers.

BzzAgent Reetl1 wrote, "On Christmas morning my parents came over for the holiday, and I always make coffee. Well, I received the Home Café on Christmas Eve and I decided to let my parents try a cup from the Café. They both loved it. My dad usually does not really comment on things like coffee but to my surprise, he absolutely loved it. He told me how great the coffee was and, believe it or not, he wants to buy one for their house. He said it was the best cup of coffee he ever had."

BzzAgent Lillian144 brewed up a cup for her friend when she stopped in. "My friend Kathy came over for a visit, and I asked her if she would like some coffee. She said don't go to the bother, it's too much trouble for just one person. I said, oh no, I got a new Home Café coffee pot and it makes one cup. She could not imagine. I made her a cup as she watched in disbelief. She marveled at how fast and easy it was. She said the taste was really the true test. Well, it passed with flying colors. Great coffee, she said."

BzzAgent rlmiles, a financial services executive, installed a machine in his company's break room. "As COO IT/MIS for the Chicago/Midwest region for American Express Financial Advisors, I am the top of the totem pole for my office. I put a Home Café machine in our departmental coffee area (next to the regular machine that spews out terrible coffee for free) with a little box that said 'ONE POD = 25 CENTS.' Before I left work today, the money box was filled with dollars and coins and almost all of the pods were gone. People love this thing! I love this thing!!!"

Even picky teenagers loved it. BzzAgent LeslieVeg wrote, "Chris, my 19-year old nephew, stopped by and told me he was on his way to Waffle House to get a cup of coffee (YUCK!). I told Chris about my new Home Café machine and showed him how it worked. He asked if it would make an iced drink. I said, sure, why not. Since I am a coffee lover and have coffee syrups (DaVinci) and flavored creamers, I set to work as I explained the machine to Chris. He wanted the 100% Colombian coffee, but a large. No problem! I had 20 oz. disposable cups and lids. I brewed (2) 9 oz. cups for him in the Home Café machine, added Irish-cream–flavored creamer and some DaVinci Chocolate Syrup, and served it over ice!!! It was gourmet!!!! He loved it! He is a college student and wants one of the Home Café machines for his dorm. I told him that cappuccino pods are available online also!! He loved that idea, since he practically lives at Starbucks!!!"

We have hundreds and hundreds of these reports. If you stacked up all the exclamation points in them, the pile would reach the space station (which could definitely benefit from a single-serve coffee pot, so as to avoid wasting water).

However, not all the reports were happy ones. Some of the agents who were accepted in the campaign sent us emails about product reviews they had read on amazon.com and other sites. They wanted to know if the Home Café System they were going to receive would be OK. Others, who had received their machines, weren't satisfied with its performance.

BzzAgent shoppingqueen wrote:

"I took the Home Café to my job. My co-workers and I unpacked it, ran a couple of water-only cycles, and then brewed coffee with the pods provided. The Home Café system was loud. We like large cups of coffee so we used 2 pods to brew 14 oz. cups. Our honest reaction? The coffee tasted horrible! The machine was loud and after brewing 4 cups, steam started emitting from the rear of the system. We love coffee at my job, we love it so much we even have 2 different types of bean grinders. We make daily runs to Krispy Kreme and Dunkin Donuts. We really, really want to like the Home Café but as it is we cannot. We discussed this at length. My co-workers and I felt the following: (1) Make the coffee maker quieter and more sturdy. (2) Improve the taste of the coffee. I really like Folgers coffee but the pods made coffee that tasted weak. We want to like the Home Café and would be eager to try/test/report on any improvements Folgers can come up with."

Although the favorable reports far outnumbered the unfavorable ones, there were enough negative comments that we decided to address the issue with the entire BzzAgent community. Keith, who was the Home Café com-dev expert, posted a comment on our blog. It said that we had received some negative comments about Home Café from agents and that we were eager to hear more comments about the product and the campaign.

We got a lot of response to the post. Some agents said their machines weren't working properly. Some said they had returned their machines to the local Wal-Mart or other retail outlet to get a store credit. These were not good signs.

But it was particularly interesting that most agents who had negative reactions to the product felt badly about sending in negative reports. They had been eager to get involved. They really wanted to like the product. Now they were upset that they didn't feel they had enough good things to say about the product.

Shoppingqueen wrote, "I gave some fairly negative feedback on the Home Café system, but I also gave what I and my co-workers felt were solid suggestions as to how the coffeemaker could be improved. I just hope that my honesty here is not misunderstood and taken to be one that's not grateful. I'm trying to really test drive products, share them with others, and give you guys real info to take back to sponsors, not just telling you 'oh it's great' when it's not. I am very pleased to be a BzzAgent and I'm also pleased that Home Café is looking for honest feedback. It shows their responsiveness to consumers and keeps their coffee in my grocery cart."

Pretty soon, as is often the case with anything that happens online, the story of the Home Café campaign was being told outside the BzzAgent community. John Moore, who built his reputation as a marketer at Starbucks and Whole Foods, and who now has an independent marketing practice and blogs on his site, brandautopsy.com, picked up the issue. (He's also a BzzAgent, which is how he knew about the campaign.)

"Ouch!" he wrote. "I am quickly losing what respect and trust I have left for BzzAgent, the company, and for the word-of-mouth pilgrims known as BzzAgents. How could BzzAgents endorse a product wrought with so many issues?"

We discussed the issue at great length and decided that John, as much as we love him and usually agree with him, was missing the point. BzzAgents are essentially early adopters. They are like a group of volunteer product testers. They want to be involved with the product before others know about it, often before it is generally available on the market. As a result, they are more than willing to accept that the product is not yet sparklyperfect. In fact, many of them like the opportunity to make suggestions for changes or improvements. That's a high level of involvement. It brings them social capital.

While the discussion continued in the blogosphere, we worked with our client to respond to the issue. Home Café marketers acted just as they should have. They explained that some of the machines had come from an early manufacturing run and may have had the kinds of imperfections that most limited-run, prelaunch products can have. The company offered to replace the machine of any agent who wasn't satisfied.

The agents were pleased with Folgers' response. Even those who had decided that the machine wasn't really for them or who hadn't warmed up to the taste of the coffee felt that Home Café was listening to them and responding well.

The Quiet Advocates Speak Up

Even so, the whining and moaning continued for awhile in the blogosphere (people take a lot of glee in jumping onto the negativity bandwagon), but it didn't take long for the positive value of negativity to appear.

First, people began to respond differently to the sharp-tongued stuff about the campaign that they were reading on brandautopsy and other sites. They defended the campaign, liked our response to the negative reports, and praised how Home Café had dealt with it all (just as Bardo defended SparklyPerfect and how some even defended the G6). They didn't really care that the product had had a few minor glitches. They cared more about the whole nature of the campaign and the experience. That feeling generated positive word-of-mouth that rubbed off on us and Home Café.

Motivated by the negative conversation they were hearing, the people who liked Home Café said they believed that Home Café was being unfairly bashed and felt that justice had to be done. They wrote that Home Café functioned perfectly well.

What was happening? The negative word-of-mouth was bringing out the Quiet Advocates, the people who liked (and, in some cases, were passionate about) the product but who hadn't yet talked it up. They were people who might not be particularly vocal by nature, or might not have articulated their opinion to themselves. Only when they felt that the product was being wronged did their opinion become clear and they then became motivated to offer their point of view. Suddenly, we were deluged with emails from Home Café supporters who wanted to create positive word-of-mouth about it. We still receive emails from happy agents, long after the campaign has ended.

Quiet Advocates (QAs) have a particular power in the world of word-of-mouth. They don't speak up as often as brand evangelists do. But, when they do talk, they may exert more influence in word-of-mouth conversations than the rabid brand evangelist. That's because the evangelist is always trying to get others to join the cult of the product, which can be off-putting. The QAs have a simpler goal in mind: they just want to set the record straight. Other people respond positively to that. When word-of-mouth is triggered by anger or frustration or a desire to see justice done, when folks get their backs up . . . watch out!

There is value in knowing that there are usually many customers who are product supporters but are not vocal about their support and that they can be awakened if and when a product comes under fire. Not only did Home Café benefit from the quiet advocacy that emerged in this campaign, BzzAgent did, too. Some critical comments caught the attention of one of our clients, Bruce Palmer, marketing director for NOLS (the National Outdoor Leadership School). We had just finished a pro bono campaign for it as part of our GoodBzz program, which offers our services free of charge to nonprofits and companies with good causes. Bruce seemed to appreciate the effectiveness of the campaign, but hadn't shared his opinion publicly. When he saw that we were being bashed, he spoke up. He wrote, in part,

"NOLS, the National Outdoor Leadership School, is in the midst of a GoodBzz (pro bono for nonprofits) campaign with Bzz-

Agent. We are one of the remarkable companies that have a long history of great word-of-mouth. 97% of our graduates indicate that they would recommend NOLS to a friend and 80% of our students first heard about NOLS from a NOLS graduate, a school guidance counselor or staff at an outdoor store. So why did we pursue the GoodBzz opportunity?"

He went on to enumerate all the good things that paying attention to word-of-mouth can do, such as enabling the company to learn a lot about itself. As the result of the word-of-mouth campaign, Bruce said that he came to realize that NOLS had not been asking for enough help from its alumni, had not been doing enough to help NOLS grads talk about their experience with others, and hadn't been communicating well enough about the benefits of the experience with prospective students.

Bruce wasn't alone. Other clients came forward and spoke up for us. Knowing that there's a community that is willing to let you be imperfect and screw up a little, so long as you include them and treat them fairly, provides a company with a license to take some risks.

The marketing world would like to think that the faults of a product or service can be hidden. But consumers search out the good and the bad and yearn to communicate about real value. Word-of-mouth will strip your product to its skivvies and show it to the world.

Phony positivity can result in negative word-of-mouth. Truthful negativity can generate positive word-of-mouth.

Weird.

Bardo the Loyalist

Fall rolls around. SparklyPerfect is performing like gang-busters. Andie ratchets down on the marketing spend—no more TV or radio. Scales back on the print campaign. The Perky Squirrel actors have hung up their furry suits. One of them has a gig as a perp on *Law and Order*.

The word-of-mouth campaign is also winding down. After twelve weeks, the SPers have connected with the main contacts in their networks. They're still keen to communicate, but there's not much SparklyPerfect news to share, so most of them have moved on to other products and services.

One crisp autumn morning, Farman calls Andie into his office.

"I've been thinking," he says.

Andie quickly checks the credenza to see if he's still under the influence of the Pilgrim's book. There it is, lying open and face down, even more clogged with stickies than before.

"You executed a great campaign," says Farman. "I've tracked everything. You got awareness. You got impressions. You got buzz. You got plenty of word-of-frigging-mouth. You nailed the PTC. Most important, you got sales. Well done."

"Thank you." Andie braces for the "but" that she knows is coming.

"However," says Farman. "Now comes the interesting part. How do we keep it going?"

"SparklyPerfect Plus is in the pipeline," says Andie. "It's only eight months away."

"In the meantime, how do we keep the consumers' enthusiasm from cooling off? How do we keep them connected with the brand? How do we keep them INVOLVED with the company?"

"We have the postpurchase focus groups planned," Andie reminds him. "We'll be doing the online survey biannually. There's the response area on the Web site."

"The real question, Andie, is this: once you've gotten the customers to buy, then what do you want them to do?" Farman gazes at her with an expression of deep marketing enquiry. "I mean, just what are customers really for?"

Bardo and Megan have spent a delightful summer exploring the joys of SparklyPerfect. They've used it a hundred times—in the kitchen, at the barbecue, and at the summer cottage.

All summer long, Bardo has done plenty of talking about SparklyPerfect. In fact, he has become the recognized neighborhood expert in all things SP. Neighbors ask him about features and compare price info with him. If he sees someone at the local home store mulling over a purchase of SP, he always offers his (positive) opinion.

But, by late September, with barbecue season over and action picking up in the dairy department, SparklyPerfect moves to Bardo's product backburner. Bardo's word-of-mouth window is starting to close.

One Saturday Bardo bumps into Cam at the coffee shop not far from his house. They sit together, Cam slurping his latte and Bardo slugging his double espresso, and chat about flat-screen TVs, hybrid cars, and freezer mitts.

An attractive couple in their midthirties enters the coffee shop. Bardo doesn't recognize them. They joke a little with the barista, order two coffees and a couple of large chocolate bars. When the drinks are ready, they take them to a table in the middle of the shop, right next to Bardo and Cam. While they settle themselves, they look around at the other patrons.

After a few sips of his cappuccino, the man taps the table as if he's just had a great idea. "Hey," he says to his companion, a blond woman in a tight fuzzy top, "let's use the new VROOM to grind the chocolate onto the top of our drinks."

"Great idea," says the woman. She reaches into her bag and brings out a shiny gizmo that looks a little like SparklyPerfect, only smaller and lighter. It is beautifully finished in matte magenta and silver colors. She turns it on and it emits a pleasant purring sound.

"Got a good charge on the battery?" the man asks her.

"Oh, yeah," she says. "This sweetheart is good for at least two hours of cordless operation."

Bardo and Cam cannot help but listen in on the conversation and watch the scene. They glance at each other. What gives?

When the woman has completed the chocolate operation and the couple is happily sipping away, the man taps the table again, seemingly with another bright idea. "Hey, do you mind if I use the VROOM to go online?"

"Not at all," she says, handing the snappy little gizmo to him. He immediately seems to be engrossed in some Web activity.

This is too much for Cam and Bardo. A cordless kitchen gadget with online capability? What the hell is this VROOM thing?

The woman notices that Bardo and Cam are looking at her and smiles. "Hi," she says.

Bardo smiles back. The woman says to him, sotto voce, as if with great confidentiality, "What can ya do?" She shrugs and gestures toward her companion. "I live for chocolate. He loves to surf."

Bardo nods knowingly. "What is that thing?" he asks.

"It's the new VROOM," she says. "We just got it."

"You can really crumble chocolate AND go online with that machine?" Cam asks.

"Sure can," she says.

"You can use it in the car, too," says the man, without looking up from the VROOM screen.

"And take it to the beach," adds the woman. "It has the sports case. Totally waterproof. Keeps out sand. Great for cookouts."

This is too much for Bardo. "Are you serious?"

She does a high-raise of the eyebrows as if to signify just how much fun can be had with VROOM at the beach.

"Want to have a look?" the man asks Bardo.

The man swivels around so that Bardo and Cam can get a better look at the VROOM. It is a sweet little unit and the Web feature is amazing.

"Where'd you get it?" asks Cam.

"I think it's only available online," says the man. "But wait a second, I think there's a direct link to its site."

In a second, they're looking at www.vroom.com.

"It's made by a French company," says the woman to Bardo. "I love the colors."

"Oh," says the man. "They're offering a special rebate deal. Twenty percent off if you buy today." The man looks at Cam. "You want to go for it?"

It's at that point that Bardo smells a rat. They've been caught in a snare. Bardo and Cam, two serious consumers, are being shilled.

"No, thanks," Bardo says. "I need to check it out a little more. Besides I already have a SparklyPerfect."

"Oh, you have one of those?" asks the woman.

"Come on, we've got to go." Bardo half-drags Cam out of the shop.

In the parking lot, Cam says, "What was that about? I was just getting into that VROOM thing."

"They were shills. Hired guns. We were being scammed."

Cam considers. He looks back into the shop. The couple is talking with another customer.

"Who cares," says Cam. "She was cute."

"I care," says Bardo. "If the company is willing to shill me, what else are they going to do?"

8

What's Next for Word-of-Mouth?

Word-of-mouth is a marketer's dream.

It's the most powerful, adaptable, fast-moving communications medium on the planet. Millions of people talking about your product—what could be more spectacular?

There's only one little problem with it: you can't measure it the way you have ever measured anything else. The reason? You can't measure the middle.

In a word-of-mouth campaign, you can measure the first interaction. Through feedback from your consumers, you can get a gauge of how many individuals have actually begun talking about the product. But after that, authentic word-of-mouth travels its own grapevine. After the first generation of consumers starts telling stories to the people in their networks, there is no way to track how many interactions take place or how many people have been involved.

Word-of-mouth is impossible to measure for many reasons. It's not scheduled. It doesn't "come on" at any exact time. You can't turn it on or turn it off. Sometimes it moves very fast. Sometimes it moves slowly. It's not contained in a single medium. It takes all kinds of forms. It's the intimate conversation between two friends on the street. It's an email string linking seventeen colleagues in five countries around the world. It's the bantering dialogue among five people at a barbecue. It's the speech presented to fifty thousand people at a stadium. It's the flurry of instant messaging between whoever is connected at that moment. It's a late-night telephone chat, a postcard from Nepal, and, yes, even that rare form of anti-quarian communication, the handwritten letter.

Word-of-mouth often is all but invisible. It happens when people observe each other in the mall or at the sales counter. There's a huge amount of information and meaning delivered in the lift of an eye-brow or the subtle chuckle.

Word-of-mouth is an infinite grapevine of bits of communica-tion in thousands of forms, which we assimilate and draw con-clusions from. How the hell can it be captured, evaluated, or measured? There are no impressions to count, no email returns to track, no mouse clicks to collect. No single measurement can ever point to the exact return of so many and such varied exchanges.

Yes, of course, that's all true, but it doesn't change the fact that we live by measurement. Everything we do in companies has to be measured. How else can we know what's working and what isn't? How can we know where to put our resources?

Word-of-mouth can accomplish so much. It can generate sales. Build loyalty. Support PR. Get someone to a store that's hidden on a weird one-way street. Foster trust. But those things aren't enough, because they're so hard to measure. And companies need measurement.

That's why I have just invented a new way to measure word-of-mouth. It's called Nano-Slips™.

Let's imagine that Bardo, and everybody else in the world, is assigned a WOMID (word-of-mouth ID). Bardo's is #1, of course, because I have just made him the first person to use the system. Because I can. (You can be #2 if you want.)

Suppose that GlobalGajitz (GG) decides that it wants to track the word-of-mouth for its SparklyPerfect launch. GG sends Bardo a little pad of paper. His WOMID, #1, is printed on each slip. The company sends a similar pad to everyone in the world, each with that person's WOMID printed on it.

Bardo takes the pad with him wherever he goes. Every time he has a word-of-mouth interaction about SparklyPerfect, he tears off a slip and gives it to the person he has just interacted with. The other person does the same in return. Now we discover that these are no ordinary, paper-and-special-glue Post-it pads. No, they are nanotech smart pads. Each slip of paper is embedded with thousands of tiny microchips that monitor the movements of the slip and automatically record the date, time, and GPS location of every interaction.

Bardo keeps all the Nano-Slips he's collected from the people he's had interactions with. They keep his. When he buys his SparklyPerfect, he hands his slips over to the store clerk or inserts them into a special reader. With the data taken from Bardo's Nano-Slips, GlobalGajitz can create an incredible analysis that shows exactly how many interactions he had about SparklyPerfect, what kind they were, whom he had them with, where, and when. Then they can integrate that info with data about their marketing activities and see how the two correlate. They can do the same for everybody else in the world. They will end up with the most astonishing measurement of any marketing media ever created.

And here's what they will find out from the analysis: not much. They'll learn that the number of word-of-mouth interactions varies wildly, based on the person and the type of purchase involved. Some people have a single point of interaction and buy the product immediately. Others have dozens and still don't buy it. For those who do buy, it will still be difficult—if not impossible—to tell exactly what medium has driven the sale. Was it the last interaction that Bardo had that pushed him over the edge? Or was it an interaction that took place earlier that he just hadn't yet acted on? They will find out that human behavior is complex and often misunderstood. Just like word-of-mouth.

They will also learn that word-of-mouth impacts every other element of the cycle and that every marketing element has an impact on word-of-mouth and that the two intertwine together in incredibly complicated ways. An ad becomes more effective when it is accompanied by word-of-mouth about the ad. Word-of-mouth is richer when there are marketing activities that stories can be based on. A coupon is more effective if the experience an individual has with it generates more word-of-mouth.

They will further see that the total number of interactions a person has is an important component of word-of-mouth effectiveness, but the value and content of those communications are more important. Initial dialogues lead to other dialogues. Just because a product has a lot of word-of-mouth doesn't mean the interactions drive significantly more purchases.

So, even with the most sophisticated, computerized system, we'd still find that the middle was too complex and subtle to measure.*

This doesn't make any difference. Clients will continue to ask for some assurance that their word-of-mouth campaign would be worth the investment. "I won't buy until you show me ROI," they will demand.

So, here's what we can say.

---

*In fact, something very like Nano-Slips has been in development for years and is now being tested: the Portable People Meter, jointly developed by Arbitron and Nielsen (!). The PPM is designed to be worn by an individual and record every interaction he or she has with a piece of specially encoded medium, such as a radio ad or TV program.

We know that word-of-mouth can and does increase sales. One way to show this is by comparing sales of a product in two similar markets: one with a word-of-mouth campaign, the other without.

In 2004, we performed a study for Wharton School Publishing (WSP) that did just this. In five cities across the United States, WSP ran a marketing campaign that included public relations, advertising, and other initiatives. In five other cities, the campaign used those same elements, but also included 1,500 volunteers who got involved in a word-of-mouth effort to experience WSP and then share their opinion of it with others. Sales in both cities were tracked for fourteen weeks. We found that in the cities with a word-of-mouth component sales were 66 percent higher during that period than in the cities without a word-of-mouth campaign.

This type of measurement provides some useful data about short-term return on investment, but it doesn't measure the overall value that word-of-mouth delivers. The product evangelist keeps on talking and the word-of-mouth keeps on rippling out through endless generations, and often continues when there is no more advertising or marketing or buzz campaign to fuel it.

BzzAgent DontheIdeaGuy says it well:

"I think the most valuable benefits of word-of-mouth come months and years down the road. An immediate bump in sales— sure. That can happen with any standard advertising effort, but what about all the people that will be influenced down the road? You cannot simply write off all future buying decisions to whatever campaign you might be running at the time—many of those decisions to buy could have been influenced by a word-of-mouth comment from a trusted source (and have nothing to do with the silly television ad you bought yesterday)."

So, it would be extremely useful to try to measure the return of an evangelist over a prolonged period of time by continuing to document their purchase behavior. That's just what we did for the One True Fit campaign that we conducted for Lee jeans in 2003. (See Chapter 6.) One thousand women participated in that campaign and the word-of-mouth they generated was impressive. For example, 88 percent of them said that the campaign had changed their perception of Lee jeans.

But it was the reports of their behavior six months later that were most powerful. Fifty percent of them said they had purchased additional pairs of Lee jeans; 16 percent said they had bought three pairs; 39 percent had bought two; and 31 percent had bought one additional pair. Eighty-three percent reported they had talked about One True Fit in the three months after the campaign had officially ended. Such results go some distance toward proving that word-of-mouth has the capability to change perceptions and increase sales long after the word-of-mouth has been initially sparked by the company.

In the end, measurement always focuses on one thing and one thing only: sales. But what about all the other value that word-of-mouth brings to a product and company? How else can the consumer dialogue contribute?

Consumers have long been thought of as targets, people whom marketers wanted to grab and gouge. But that's over. Consumers have way too much money, knowledge, access, and choice to settle for being targets. They're drunk on the power they now have.

But fear not! With all that skill and knowledge and power, consumers are becoming a resource the company can, and should, tap into. They have the skills and interest in gathering and disseminating product information. They help decide if you need to refresh your packaging and bring out the next generation of the product. They are helping to make decisions because they tell you if you've made the right ones.

Who Gets the Customer?

Some companies understand the new view of what the customer is for. Some don't.

Coca-Cola didn't. In the summer of 2004, Coke launched a new low-carb, low-cal beverage called C2. The launch campaign was, according to *AdAge,* Coke's most expensive advertising roll-out in twenty-two years. The last brand they spent so much money on was Diet Coke.

Even before the first marketing dollar was spent, it was clear that the Coca-Cola Company was repeating some of the same mistakes it made with the launch of New Coke back in 1985. According to the March 26, 2004, issue of *Beverage Digest,* Coke would soon release the product, but preferred to keep consumers in the dark about just what the product would be. (A scooter that couldn't tip over?) Its internal code name: Project Freedom.

No doubt years of research had gone into developing the product and countless focus groups had been sipping away and trying to describe to researchers what their taste buds were telling them. But Coke and its bottlers told the press that an important element of the campaign would be to educate consumers about "what these products are." In other words, Coke viewed the consumer as a target, an uninformed bunch who would need to be "taught" about the glory of the new beverage. Instead of having a dialogue with consumers, Coke's plan was to train them.

Coke also neglected to include in its launch another very important word-of-mouth community of influence: its employees. These are people who talk about their experiences as part of their everyday life. They share issues about co-workers. They chat about what it is they are working on with family and friends and co-workers. They influence each other. Their identity is partially derived from their work experience. Sure, the marketers knew what they were attempting. The months they spent in development involved late nights, long hours, and angry spouses. But the company as a whole was so in the dark, C2 being the biggest secret of the decade, that they didn't have a chance to get behind it.

Not only did Coke keep its employees in the dark, it ignored its bottlers, as well. These people talk to Coca-Cola executives, who listen as co-workers but also as consumers. They talk to their wives and husbands and to their friends, who always want the scoop on what Coke is up to next. They talk to their distributors, who talk to the press, who talk to bloggers. Why not provide them with good information about what the product is all about?

The day C2 was launched, Coke issued the following statement: "'Consumers are the true architects of this idea,' said Doug Daft, chairman and chief executive officer, The Coca-Cola Company. 'Coca-Cola C2 was created to specifically address their desire for a lower-calorie cola with that great Coca-Cola taste.'" If consumers were the true architects of the idea, then how come they spent their time guessing and being confused about the product?

The launch was a miracle of coordination, integration, and cleverness. TV ads used music from the Rolling Stones and Queen. There was presence on radio, outdoors, movies, and on-line. The campaign's tagline: "1/2 the carbs. 1/2 the cals. All the great taste."

Unfortunately, despite all the TV roadblocks, incredible click-throughs, and huge number of impressions made, C2 bombed.

The irony of this is that Coke is a company that is highly capable of generating positive word-of-mouth about their product. They have consumers who fervently believe in their brand. Those individuals, who had supported Coca-Cola for years, were not about to become C2 evangelists upon their first hearing of the

Queen song. They might have been convinced, however, if Coke had asked for the engagement and their support. All Coke had to do was ask. Instead, the company told.

In January 2005, just six months after the release of C2, Coca-Cola announced a restructuring of its North American division to pull itself out of a sales slump. In addition, the veteran chief marketing officer, Javier Benito, resigned (was canned?). Analysts speculated that he was paying the price for the C2 debacle.

Coca-Cola had a huge opportunity to make C2 a success. Consumers ultimately rejected it because they didn't see its distinctive value. The supporters of the brand didn't feel engaged in the launch, but instead felt like targets to the massive marketing machine that is Coca-Cola.

Coke didn't get the new role of the consumer dialogue, but many companies do.

Take, for example, our first client, Penguin Group. After running many book marketing campaigns for them, we found that we were receiving vast amounts of feedback from consumers about what they liked and didn't like about the books, most of it through their BzzAgent reports. They told us not just how they had Bzzed the book, but about how they thought it might have been better, about thoughts on the title, and about the other marketing efforts surrounding the book.

We know that agents like taking part in campaigns because they like being listened to. But we didn't know at that time that many agents wanted their opinions to count for more and to have more influence with the company. When we received reports that offered comments and suggestions, we responded to the agents, saying how much we appreciated their ideas, and told them we'd pass them along to the publisher. But that did not really involve the consumer in the process.

So Rick Pascocello, our client at Penguin, agreed to allow the advocates into the process. We ran a poll asking agents to help us choose a title for a Penguin book about JetBlue, the airline. We gave them two titles to choose from and the option to express why they liked their choice. They could also suggest other ideas. We offered the survey to about four thousand volunteers. Within twenty-four hours we had more than two thousand responses. Some people just clicked on the title they liked best, but many took the time to write long rationales about why one title was better than another. Seventy percent of them chose *Blue Streak: Inside jetBlue, the Upstart That Rocked an Industry,* and that's what Portfolio went with. The volunteers loved being involved in the process, even if their choice was not the final one.

WITH versus AT Marketing

So, you can't really measure the effect of word-of-mouth, but you want to bring the consumer dialogue closer to the core of the company, and always give the consumer something to talk about.

That suggests a new approach to marketing that more fully incorporates word-of-mouth. I call it WITH marketing, as opposed to the traditional AT marketing. (AT marketing is about targeting, capturing, and one-way communication.) WITH marketing means that companies and consumers work with each other. They cease to think of consumers as targets. They find ways to let them in the door and partner with them. In WITH marketing you don't talk about capturing. You talk about listening. Targeting is a concept from the days of old. Now it's about engaging.

The era of WITH marketing involves blurring the lines between the consumer and the company. No longer is it solely about the marketer saying, "This is how I will market to you." Nor is it solely about the consumer saying, "This is how I'm going to share my experiences with a product with my friends only." WITH marketing is a combination of the two.

Patagonia, which we discussed in Chapter 6, is a WITH marketing company. Patagonia had been built on word-of-mouth but, over the years, had done very little to understand how its grapevine worked, gather data about it, or think about how it might engage with its consumers more. So, Craig Wilson partnered with a former employee, Anthony Schweizer, who was attending the Kingston School of Business in London, to study what it was that made ordinary consumers into raving Patagoniacs. They learned that Patagonia has a fundamentally customer-centric model, based on the idea that many people have their first interaction of the brand through another person, rather than through an ad or a piece of marketing communications. A young person, for example, might get introduced to the brand by an older family member. Craig likes to say, "People enter into a relationship with Patagonia by a recommendation, which carries greater weight than if you enter into it on your own."

They also learned that Patagonia's iron-clad guarantee helps keep customers loyal. ("We guarantee everything we make. If you are not satisfied with one of our products at the time you receive it, or if one of our products does not perform to your satisfaction, return it to the store you bought it from or to Patagonia for a repair, replacement or refund. Damage due to wear and tear will be repaired at a reasonable charge.") Even though some people seemed to be abusing the guarantee by returning loads of merchandise or seeking replacement of stuff they had just whacked the bejesus out of, it didn't matter. Even the abusers were generating word-of-mouth that was far more valuable than the cost of replacing the clothes. But, of course, Patagonia had had no way of quantifying this.

A survey of about four hundred Patagonia customers showed

that people's recommendations of the brand, often involving Patagonia's iron-clad guarantee, increase with the length of the consumer's tenure with the brand. In other words, the more time a customer spends with the brand, the more they'll communicate about it with others as time goes along. So, the company's tolerance of the guarantee abusers seemed to be increasing the willingness of the abusers to recommend the Patagonia brand to others.

The question that Patagonia now faces, as do all companies, is how to further engage its loyal customers. Wilson and his colleagues do not fundamentally believe in creating a sparklyperfect "marketing story." Rather, they take a Zenlike approach to their brand. They think about continually defining who they are and positioning themselves to become what they want to be. If they execute well on those ideas, consumers will continue to engage with the Patagonia brand—appreciating what it is and helping it to evolve to the next stage.

How to best engage the consumer is a question that we are always considering for our clients and something that we always think about in our own community. That's why we got BzzAgents involved in the development of this book. Starting in early 2005, we offered BzzAgents the capability to help us define the product you're reading right now. They saw early jacket designs, title choices, and bits of content. They were instrumental in helping us understand what it is they really wanted from a book about word-of-mouth. These individuals represent one subset of the population who we hope will read the book, but this is a book about them and—much more important—a book they've invested themselves in over the years. Without their help and participation, we wouldn't have realized that stealth marketing is a no-win game for consumers and companies alike. We wouldn't have recognized the weird power of negativity. We wouldn't have seen that everyday people are the real evangelists for products. And we wouldn't have understood that the reasons people communicate with others about products and services are deeply human, rather than materialistic, ones.

BzzAgent itself provides a glimpse of a new kind of WITH marketing world in which the consumer plays a lead role and the company is not obsessed with force-feeding them messages and using sparklyperfect tactics to influence them to make a purchase. In fact, we are currently developing such platforms for many companies that have large groups of consumer bases and want to be able to engage with them in new ways.

WITH communities could also be built in not-for-profit, educational, and government organizations, even though they don't strictly make a product or have consumers. Consider the U.S. armed forces, for example. In 2005, the armed forces were having trouble attracting new recruits for many reasons, including the possibility of prolonged and hazardous service in Iraq. The news media were filled with stories about how difficult it was for recruiters to connect with people and "sell them" on joining up and getting involved. A typical scene showed a couple of crisply uniformed sergeants approaching a group of kids outside a mall or on a school campus. The kids are wearing baggy jeans, and they're listening to the recruiters as if they were being scolded by the principal at school. The kids stare at the pavement and steal glances across the street. They would obviously rather be anywhere else doing anything else but this. They don't relate to the two recruiters. They don't like being sold. They hate feeling pressured. They don't know these guys and they don't want to know them.

Even the recruiters feel the stress. They don't like hanging around malls looking for likely prospects and chasing after them like used-car salesmen. Even though it's unmistakable who they are, the recruiters feel like shill marketers—telling a hyped-up story to unwitting targets. It's a no-win game for both sides. It's a constant struggle, because street recruitment is a form of AT marketing. The news stories reveal that the recruiters dislike their jobs so much that they suffer from depression, sign up ineligible candidates just to meet their monthly quotas, and often try to get other duty. Some even say they would prefer to be in combat rather than be a recruiter.

It must be obvious to the armed forces that their form of AT marketing is not working. But what if the armed forces took a WITH way? What if they formed a WITH community? What if they talked with their own people about how they think and feel about service in the military? What if wives and kids of soldiers had a voice? What if all aspects of military service could be discussed? And if the armed services could really listen and respond to the incredible amounts of word-of-mouth that are already out there about everything associated with the armed forces—and help the community talk with its members more effectively?

It sounds like a huge and unlikely undertaking, I admit. The U.S. government creating a WITH community with the Army, Air Force, Navy, and Marines? The U.S. government listening to word-of-mouth? But just imagine what might change for the better if it could.

The key is that organizations of all types have to think differently about how they're going to engage with their own community as it relates to their goals. BzzAgent has proven that consumers want to be involved. It's up to the company to involve them in a way that's effective, and to treat them as part of the system—as part of the very engine that makes them go.

Deception Kills Word-of-Mouth

There are some observers—and very smart and insightful ones, at that—who see the BzzAgent phenomenon quite differently than we do. In fact, they think we're quite evil. William Gibson, author of the fabulous book *Pattern Recognition,* is one of them. After reading the *New York Times* article about us ("The Hidden (In Plain Sight) Persuaders," December 5, 2004), and receiving requests from fans to explain his vision of a consumer-driven world, he wrote:

"Let me get this straight. Because I imagined, without knowing that BzzAgent existed, that this sort of thing not only could but would be done, the fact that BzzAgent exists makes me 'paranoid'? Or is it merely the imagining that makes me 'paranoid'? *Pattern Recognition* isn't 'about a future,' of course, and the present reality, judging by this piece, is one in which corporations have become so powerful that they can recruit unpaid volunteers to infiltrate your life and talk up products—a twist I evidently wasn't quite paranoid enough to imagine."

Gibson's comments were mild in comparison to those of David Byrne, he of Talking Heads fame and now a general observer of popular culture and modern life. On his blog he wrote, "An article in the *Times* magazine section on a couple of companies who specialize in word-of-mouth marketing campaigns. These are campaigns, paid for by corporate clients, to raise the awareness and profile of a product by getting a small army of 'agents' to drop a mention of the product into casual conversation, carry it (in the case of a book) prominently displayed on the subway, write reviews to Amazon, ask for the product at shops, all without revealing that one is promoting it. It's a Philip K. Dick world. There are tens of thousands of these 'agents' out there. Ordinary people, not necessarily trendsetters or celebrities, who are living breathing advertisements . . . and proud of it. We don't know, for example, when someone is merely being helpful or informative, or even friendly, or when they have a hidden agenda. When they're slipping a bit of product placement into the conversation and when they're just engaging in the occasional mention of a book or brand as part of normal everyday life. So, in this world, which is our world, no one is to be trusted. No one's word, on this stuff at least, is to be taken at face value?"

But both Byrne and Gibson are missing the boat, and Byrne, one of my personal idols as a teen, is dramatically wrong with his assumption that BzzAgents are anonymous "stealth" marketers. Neither of them really gets what BzzAgent is all about. Their natural inclination is to assume that the word-of-mouth marketing process only and always works through deception. They don't see that, when there is full transparency and the system is based on the honest sharing of genuine opinions, word-of-mouth can be harnessed without it becoming a nightmare world of paranoid fantasies and secret agents lurking inside your brain. It all comes back to the natural inclination of people to talk about products. Remember, we found that 14 to 27 percent of all word-of-mouth interactions include some kind of reference to products or services. People talk about products all the time. Everybody does it and everybody knows it. Does the fact that they're consciously helping the company through the sharing of their honest opinion make them untrustworthy?

Unfortunately, there are some companies out there whose activities do fit Gibson's nasty vision of word-of-mouth marketing. They don't believe in transparency and don't get the idea of engaging their customers. But, even worse, there are companies and marketers and individuals who spend their time and energy attempting to subvert the natural and positive power of that engagement. They have a variety of methods for their devious purposes. They lurk in chat rooms. They pose as everyday consumers. They pay moderators of forums, blogs, and other online communities to embed content that looks and sounds truthful but is biased or incorrect. They hire actors to engage with consumers in scripted conversations without being forthright about their true identities and who is backing them.

If such practices continue, they could damage the very fabric of word-of-mouth. Companies will have little chance to build partnerships with their customers. In conversation, people will feel more distrust for each other's motives. Is a shill marketer lurking inside the skin of every person I meet?

The power of word-of-mouth lies in its honesty. It lies in the fact that it is about real and transparent opinions—both good and bad. Consumers continue to rely on the credibility of their friends', family's, and acquaintances' opinions because they are pure and without manipulation.

Although word-of-mouth is the oldest form of marketing communications, it is becoming more important than ever, primarily because people have come to almost completely distrust the marketing messages they see and hear every day. We see deception and condescension everywhere. In the advertorials that look like magazine articles to make them seem more reputable. In the government's video news releases that are dressed up to look like network reports. In the pop-up ads that scream at us to click because our computer may have a computer virus. Spammers are constantly adjusting their messages to make us think that we've been approved for a mortgage or can get cheap prescription medicine or can enlarge a body part. Ad agencies put their creative teams to work building fake blogs and releasing anonymous viral videos. Record labels and television studios distribute material on open-source networks and then claim it was stolen from them. We've been well trained by marketers not to believe any of their communications. That is why, more and more, we search out the truth about products and services through word-of-mouth.

The irony is that the organizations that use these misleading and deceptive means to try to harness word-of-mouth get far less return than if they nurtured word-of-mouth and helped it become stronger by listening to and engaging with the real opinions of real consumers.

When we first developed the BzzAgent model, we asked the members of our community not to reveal that they were agents. But it didn't work. The agents just kept telling others that they were agents. They did so because they understood that you can't have real word-of-mouth without real openness and transparency. They were willing to communicate with others about their opinions about a product, but only if those opinions were their own real, personal opinions. They didn't want to be thought of as covert operators or to have to sneak around in any way. In fact, they liked telling people they were agents, and still do. It's all part of the word-of-mouth process. The agents taught us to think differently. Now we make sure that everyone knows to be completely open about their involvement with BzzAgent.

There are truthful offers and truthful advertisers. But they've become burdened with the transgressions of others. As a result, we've chosen to place our trust elsewhere: in the opinions of our neighbors, friends, co-workers, family members—even strangers. And, as I hope we've shown in this book, that's exactly where our trust belongs.

Let's protect the future and build something sustainable. Every marketer who seeks to harness word-of-mouth should engage in honest practices. (Your clients will grow your businesses.) Every company should seek the support of its consumers instead of fooling them. (You'll win more evangelists this way.) And every individual should refuse to be paid for deceiving fellow consumers. (You'll sleep easier at night.)

And so will I.

Final Review

After six months on the market, the launch of SparklyPerfect officially comes to an end.

"And what did we learn from all this?" Farman asks Andie. "What do we know now that we didn't know before?"

"Well," Andie says. "We learned it's difficult to quantify the ROI of Perky Squirrel characters."

Farman doesn't laugh.

"What about the word-of-mouth campaign?" he asks.

Andie pauses for a moment. "We learned that people were talking about SP all the time. Much more than we'd ever imagined. And in different ways."

"How so?"

"They talked about the media almost as much as they talked about the product. They mentioned the print ads, which I didn't expect. And, of course, they talked about the pasta accessory problem and how we responded to it."

"Is it possible to calculate a word-of-mouth ROI?"

Andie scratches her head. "We have piles of data. But I wouldn't say I could come up with a hard number."

"So should I recommend that we don't fund word-of-mouth activities in the future?"

Pregnant pause.

"I believe the word-of-mouth campaign helped build sales," says Andie. "Even though I can't really quantify by how much."

Andie tries to imagine a future campaign WITHOUT a word-of-mouth component. She can't. "But we got a huge return on other things," she says, with new conviction.

"Such as?"

"Knowledge," she says. "We gained a lot of knowledge about the product itself and how people use it and think about it. That's valuable."

"Yes."

"Plus, consumer engagement. Loyalty. Evangelism. Whatever you want to call it."

"How do we know that?"

"Because the geographic areas where we had the strongest word-of-mouth also had the strongest response to other media, particularly direct mail and coupons."

"Aha!" Farman is obviously pleased. "So it's the integration of media? Each communication is a conversation, right? Not just a quick flash of light on the retina. People need the kind of data and credibility they get from a conversation to decide whether they're gonna buy."

Andie inclines her head. "Maybe."

"Well, if you accept that," Farman continues, "isn't the value that we can get more long-term engagement from our consumer relationships and greater value from our communications? That we can really bake the consumer into the brand?"

"I'm not sure," says Andie. But she suspects that Farman already has a vision in mind.

"What if we could build some kind of permanent platform?" asks Farman rhetorically. "A community of Global-Gajitz consumers. Pull back the curtains and bring them inside."

"Interesting idea," says Andie. She remembers word-of-mouth reports from many consumers saying they would like to help in some way, to be more involved.

"Your new assignment," says Farman, "is to become our very own in-house GlobalGajitz word-of-mouth expert."

Andie smiles gamely. "I'm in," she says. "But can I still do taxi toppers?"

"Sure," says Farman. "Word-of-mouth does not NECESSARILY mean the end of marketing as we know it."

Meanwhile, SparklyPerfect has become an important member of Bardo's family. Bardo, Megan, and Lily refer to it colloquially as SP, as in "Don't you think it's time to haul out the old SP and fire up the barbecue?"

Bardo has watched as the competitive gadget, VROOM, has come onto the market. But he has heard (through the grapevine) that the online performance is not all it's cracked up to be. (How could a kitchen gadget really double as a wireless Internet access device?) Not only that, it isn't totally waterproof and when water seeps in, it can konk out, which is a bummer when you're using it at the beach, miles from home.

So, Bardo sticks with SparklyPerfect and turns his attention to other products. In particular, he likes the look of a new type of freezer mitt, featuring a solar-powered XM radio receiver.

And what of the Word-of-Mouth Pilgrim? He finishes his book. It becomes a modest international best-seller. He appears on *Oprah*. He advises heavyweight business executives, presidents and prime ministers, media moguls, and sports icons around the world. But no matter how globally famous he gets, he never stops listening to the dialogue of everyday people about products and services, or asking why and how they talk about them. And he never stops trying to learn about the most amazing communications medium the world has ever known: word-of-friggin'-mouth.

Grapevine

THE NEW ART OF WORD-OF-MOUTH MARKETING

FROM THE CEO
AND FOUNDER OF
BzzAgent

Dave Balter & John Butman

Why the second cover?

This is the cover that 15,000 BzzAgents chose for Grapevine. Some thought it would get shelved in the wine section, so it didn't make the final cut.

But we love it anyway.

So we put it here as a way to thank the Bzz-Agents for sharing their honest opinion. It really counts!

Deep Inside the Hive: More Reports from the BzzAgents

What follows are several BzzReports, chosen by the people who interact with the agents 24/7—the BzzAgent staff members. With each report, we've included the name of the staffer who chose it and the reason he or she thought it was worth including. They represent a sample of the kinds of activities that still get us talking—after 200,000 reports—in the Central Hive (A.K.A. the BzzAgent offices). The reports also reveal more about how real people interact with products they love. And, quite simply, they can be addictive to read. Enjoy!

Staffer: Keith Leong, Associate Copy Editor
BzzCampaign: Home Café
Reason for Choosing: Since there wasn't a report about penguins or *MacGyver*, I decided to go with this one since it's sweet. I also like dolphins. Hi, Mom!

BzzAgent jenniferrich Reports:
A lady I work with, Sharon, is going through a rough time. She has 3 young children—8, 6, and 1. Her husband left her last month

(the week before Christmas) to run off with some woman he met on a chat room playing on the Internet. He managed to max out their credit cards and clean out their bank account on his way out of town. She has been having an extremely tough time financially making ends meet. Before her husband left, Sharon would come into work each morning with her cup of Starbucks or Dunkin Donuts coffee. She loves a good cup of coffee! That was the one "extra" thing she always provided for herself. Now, Sharon is starting her day with the stale coffee we serve at work. I asked Sharon to run to Wal-mart with me during our lunch hour, just to keep me company. I had been thinking about something special I could do to help her through all this. Walking into Wal-mart today, I knew what that thing would be. Wal-mart had a clearance rack up at the front of the store and on the top shelf I saw a Home Café coffee maker. It was marked down to $29.95! Being a frugal coupon shopper that I am, I remembered I had a $10 off coupon with me. Great—only $20! I told Sharon that I was getting this for her so she could have her "extras" again! Sharon can have the wonderful taste of Starbucks in her own home and in less than 1 minute. Tears welled up in her eyes. She said "people have been helping me in so many ways but no one has been as thoughtful as you to know what makes me happy—I do miss my good coffee!" We were both crying and hugging each other. An older lady was standing next to us and said "wow that must be some deal—what is it?" So, we explained our story and she put a coffee maker in her cart as well. To make this deal even sweeter, I remembered the $20 rebate. I just filled it out and sent it in using Sharon's name and address. She will be surprised in a few weeks to get an extra $20 in the mail! What a great feeling to make someone's day!

Staffer: Jovan Hsu, Associate Producer
BzzCampaign: Castrol SYNTEC

Reason for Choosing: It's the best when we put a quality product in the hands of an expert who really knows how to Bzz. A natural and effective Bzz and a perfectly written report make this a winner. My favorite part is where he admits that he's sponsored by Valvoline but uses SYNTEC in his personal vehicles!

BzzAgent Trunkmonkey Reports:
I'm a team owner and driver for Trunkmonkey Racing, a New England–based motorsports team, and I was out in my detached garage this afternoon preparing one of our Subaru Impreza rally cars for the upcoming Ice Racing season that will be starting in a few weeks. Since we're in a residential neighborhood, I have a large Subaru race team banner hung on the front of our garage so visitors know which driveway to pull into. Over the past three years that we've lived here I get the occasional neighbor or complete stranger who wanders into the garage out of curiosity while I'm working on one of the rally cars. Today was one of those days; the sound of air tools and violent banging enticed a passer-by who rather startled me when they cheerfully said "hello" while I was underneath the car intently ratcheting away. I had just finished removing the skid plates and body armor from the bottom of the vehicle and was about to change the motor, transmission, and differential oil. My newfound friend Jason asked if he could hang around and watch, so I had him grab a case of Valvoline MaxLife off the shelf while I slid the oil pan under the car. Now here's where it gets interesting; I'm contingency sponsored by Valvoline so I now exclusively use their brand in the rally car. Next to the case of Valvoline, however, were three cases of Castrol Syntec since I'm a long-time religious Syntec user in my wife's VW Bug Turbo, my Ford Explorer service truck, and my Subaru Legacy. There's also a large metal Syntec advertising plaque hung up on the wall that I got from Exeter Subaru (shhh, don't tell Valvo-

line). It piqued Jason's curiosity as to why I had the cases of Syntec and the sign on the wall yet I was putting Valvoline in the race car, and it was about this time that I started thinking about Bzz-Agent. I explained my contingency sponsorship requirements and perks (free product and prize money) but that I used Syntec in all my other vehicles for its longevity and ability to eliminate valve knock, a well-documented but harmless quirk where Subaru 2.2 and 2.5 motors emanate a tapping noise for the first few minutes on mornings where the temperature dips below freezing. We finished the oil change on the motor, transmission, and differential and, as I was bolting the skid plates and body armor back up, Jason said that his car needed an oil change and he never realized just how easy it was! When he mentioned he drove a Subaru Forester and the Subaru banner on the garage is what actually caught his eye, I graciously offered to bring my tools and a spare set of ramps over to his house down the street. Not only did he take me up on my offer, but he actually purchased a Subaru OEM oil filter and 5 quarts of Castrol Syntec—from me!

Staffer: Kurt Overberg, Chief Technology Officer
BzzCampaign: Fantastik OxyPower
Reason for Choosing: I like this one because it's SO Real and it includes dog vomit.

BzzAgent RanchMom Reports:
I had a couple contact me regarding one of the horses I have for sale and they came by the house to look at the horse. After they'd seen the horse, they came inside to look at the horse's pedigree. While they were in my office looking over the paperwork, my two children came running through the house with their cups full of orange soda. As often happens with two children under 4 years old, they both managed to spill some of their soda (of

course they were spill proof cups, ha ha!) on my pretty white office carpet. I immediately snatched up their cups and ran to the kitchen for my bottle of Fantastik (which I've been keeping on the counter since I received it!) and a damp cloth. I sprayed the Fantastik on the stains and waited just a few minutes, while answering the couple's questions regarding pedigree. They don't have children, so they thought it was kinda funny that my kids would spill on my carpet! I didn't think it was so funny, but after a minute or two, I wiped up the stain with a damp cloth and PRESTO! The stain just disappeared! The lady commented that she thought I'd have to scrub and possibly even steam clean the area. She seemed genuinely surprised that it came up with minimal effort. I gave her some of the general info about Fantastik, mentioning that it had "oxy power" and that I especially liked that it was non-toxic.

No more than 5 minutes went by before my Brittany Spaniel came heaving through the house and, wouldn't you know it, she threw up her Alpo at the feet of the couple in my office! Again, my pretty, new, WHITE carpet was covered in an awful stain. It was disgusting and it smelled TERRIBLE! I was seething inside at this point. I really wanted to sell this couple the horse they came to look at but I hardly had started talking to them before the "incidents" began! SO, again, I ran to the kitchen, grabbed the Fantastik and the same wet rag I'd used just a few minutes before, and ran back to the scene of the "crime." After picking up the larger chunks with some paper towels, I sprayed the stain, heavily, with the Fantastik and again proceeded to wait a few minutes. We were all remarking on the terrible smell and what might have caused the dog to throw up the food she just ate. It wasn't long before the couple both commented on how well the Fantastik's nice smell covered up the nasty odor of the dog's mess. After a few minutes, I got down on all fours and scrubbed the spot with the wet cloth and again, the stain came right up. The thus-far-quiet husband remarked that he just couldn't believe how well "that stuff" worked. He told his wife to get some next time she went shopping, because they too have a farm and several dogs in their house. I promptly wrote down the Web address for them and told them that they could get a coupon there, but over-all, it was a lot less expensive than other all purpose cleaners. I told her about all the different places I've used it and how well I liked it. They seemed genuinely interested in purchasing a bottle. They decided to think about the horse for a few days before making a decision. So yay for Fantastik and boo for me! I sold a bottle of Fantastik, but not the horse!

Staffer: Kristen Beveridge, VP, Strategy & Development
BzzCampaign: Ralph Cool
Reason for Choosing: Here is my favorite report from Ralph Cool, because it is just amazing how much an agent will share with us (even things we would rather not know!).

BzzAgent renoir Reports:
My girlfriend and I went to a bar to have a few drinks and I ended up being a "naughty girl." Since you do not know me, I feel OK telling you about this. We were sitting at the bar sipping our drinks when a cutie came up beside me and asked "What are you wearing? You smell delicious." I replied "Cool, by Lauren." He then said (as he put his face next to my neck and under my long hair), "Hmm, cool, well Cool makes me hot." We then went on to have more drinks and we ended up having a very late night together, in all ways. I mean all ways. He told me the next morning he liked it enough to buy for his WIFE! But, he would think of me whenever he smelled it. Wish my name was Lorena Bobbit at that point, but live and learn.

Staffer: Tim Lash, Account Director
BzzCampaign: National Outdoor Leadership School
Reason for Choosing: This is a typical report for GoodBzz, our company's pro bono partnership with nonprofit organizations such as the National Outdoor Leadership School.

BzzAgent Keddy Reports:
My husband and I went to Gander Mountain looking for hunting equipment. I saw a "friend of a friend" & her husband and we started chatting. I thought, "what a perfect time to bring up my latest Bzz campaign." They were buying equipment to go hiking/backpacking at one of our local rock climbing areas, Nelson Ledges. I asked them if they've ever heard of the National Outdoor Leadership School or NOLS for short? Neither had. As I know most of my friends & their friends to be the outdoors type I explained what it was and the chances they'd get to be "one with nature." They generally seemed interested and not just to be nice. I explained it's not one of those "fly by" places, they've been around almost 40 years! "There's backpacking, sailing, rock climbing and even snowboarding! It has that much variety to offer!" I knew the rock climbing would bring them in, but wanted to expand their choices. Also, with the wife being very into nature, recycling, animal preserving etc., I explained the leave-no-trace philosophy they have! Unfortunately I didn't have my material for NOLS with me, however we exchanged phone numbers and we're getting together Saturday for lunch so they may view the material! I also sparked the interest of another customer that was standing nearby who asked me about this, and I invited her to meet us at the local coffee house, Mocha House, to learn more! Not only did I get to Bzz about this program and have them wanting more, my husband and I got invited to go to Nelson Ledges with them next weekend to hike along :) A truly good

experience overall. Plus, the husband does camp work during the summer months and I suggested he take the materials with him for his co-workers to review. What better place to gain more experience for camp than at NOLS?

Staffer: Val Alderson, Research Analyst
BzzCampaign: Kayem Al Fresco Chicken Sausage
Reason for Choosing: I chose this report because the agent has an amusing writing style—I like a report that makes me laugh. It also demonstrates an agent taking a chance on a new product and in turn changing the perception of his peers.

BzzAgent VeeJay Reports:
Was invited to a barbeque this weekend; everyone brings something and friends just sit around and eat and talk. I used to be the person who just brought hot dogs or sodas to these kind of cookouts. But not anymore. Not since I started buying Al Fresco sausages. Today I stopped by my local Harris-Teeter and bought some jalapeno sausages! Something nice and yummy and spicy! When I got to the party, I told the host and a bunch of people who were gathered around the grill that Al Fresco sausages are made from chicken and are so delicious and so good for you too. Much healthier than pork sausage. A couple of the people looked skeptical. This is the south, after all, where most people think that if it ain't pork, it ain't real food! So, the sausages go on the grill and as they cook they start getting golden brown and plump. Boy did they look and smell great. I noticed all of those chicken sausage skeptics were sure eyeballing the Al Fresco sausages with hungry looks in their eyes. To give credit where it's due, even the skeptics took a sausage. And after they wolfed down the Al Fresco jalapeno sausage, they took another. Glad I brought 5 packs to the party. People asked where I found the Al Fresco sausages, and

were they really made from chicken? People really seemed to love them. They sure as heck ate them up. Everyone who asked, I told them they could find them at Harris-Teeter in the fresh chicken section. I told them that any way you might cook and serve pork sausage, why you can cook and serve Al Fresco sausages the same way. Once again, Al Fresco Sausages won people over. I haven't found a soul who doesn't like them.

Staffer: Cheyanne Baird, Communications Specialist
Campaign: Tom Peters's *Project04*
Reason for Choosing: I chose this report because this agent may be Bzzing another agent. Fascinating.

BzzAgent MekaMillstone Reports:
I was speaking with the visual director of our company and noticed she had this book *Unstuck* sitting on her desk—it looked interesting so I asked her about it and she said it was basically a book for generating creativity. So I told her I recently heard that Tom Peters had released a similar type of thing for design projects. She had not heard of Tom Peters, so I explained his background. I told her I thought a lot of his work would be right up her alley especially his work with design. When I received my Tom Peters Design & Beauty Cards this week, I brought them into work to share them with her. She was very excited to look through them and is now thinking of getting her own! She loves this kind of stuff and was very excited that I had introduced her to the world of Tom Peters's work.

Staffer: Mary Del Aguila, Communications Specialist, Hispanic Channel
BzzCampaign: Wrigley's Big Red & Winterfresh Gum
Reason for Choosing: I chose this one because I think it's quite

anecdotal and represents how Bzzing can form bonds and deliver emotional rewards.

BzzAgent Waldork90 Reports:
I was at a party with some friends, but there were some kids there that I didn't know as well. We were all dancing, and my best friend said I had really good breath, and could I give him whatever I had. I guess it was slightly random, but it turned into a good Bzz. I gave him a piece of the Big Red gum, and he loved it. We've liked each other for a while, and that night, while we were dancing during a slow song, he leaned down and kissed me. This was an awesome kiss; our lips were tingling. I assume the gum had something to do with it—or at least that's what I told my friends at another house later where we were all sleeping over. This was about 10 girls. Later, four of them came back to me at different times and said that they had had great kisses as well, their boyfriends loved the sensation, and could they have more? Including 4 of my friends' boyfriends (that I heard from), about 10 girls, and my boyfriend, this is probably my biggest Bzz ever. *sigh* I love gum. :)

Staffer: Aaron Cohen, Finance and Administrative Coordinator
BzzCampaign: Comcast G4
Reason for Choosing: This is my favorite because macpgm was the first BzzAgent we spent a lot of time talking about.

BzzAgent macpgm Reports:
Alright, my friends and I sort of run the school Web site. During days that we are updating the site and such we usually—when we take it down for a few hours at a time—we put up one of those "Sorry under construction" notices up. Well my friends and I decided that we should try something different today. Sort of in-

spired by pop-up ads, my extremely computer savvy friend made a short deal in the html that forwards people from the school site to G4. Since every kid's computer automatically goes to the school site when they boot up the Internet, they now went to the G4 site. We did this in the morning because middle schoolers and high schoolers are usually in the same room together and it would be most effective. With the 35 computers in the mac labs and the 10 in the library, we uploaded the site. Since we are doing legit work to the school site, the teachers don't have a problem with it. In fact the computer teacher loves games and he was really excited when we told him about G4, I might let him borrow the DVD. So basically from 7:30–12:30 the school site should still be under construction, unless my friends update it faster than normal, but they are lazy. I sat in the lab for about 15 min when we updated it and then the students came in. I think I must have heard at least 10 kids ask what it was and looked and knew about it. I think it has been my 2nd most successful Bzz on this campaign, overall I think that at least 50 kids will know about G4, if not more. We only update the site twice a week, so maybe later in the week we will do the same. The computer teacher is being chill to let us do this, because when teachers log in they don't have to do the same internet setup, so it's just between us and the computer teacher. All I have to say is that this is somewhat revenge of the nerds in that we have the power to do this for good. Anywho peace.

Staffer: Rob Toof, Program Development Specialist
BzzCampaign: Kellogg's Smorz
Reason for Choosing: When you've read over 150,000 BzzReports, you always love a BzzReport that makes you laugh. Everyday, BzzAgents surprise us with fun stories that make our job incredibly enjoyable.

BzzAgent odiedogg Reports:
Talking with a friend about Smorz before school today. I'm out of free Smorz so I can't dish the snacks anymore, but I'm still trying to talk it up. Just because you all were so cool to make with the free cereal and stuff, even if the boxes were kinda small. Free cereal rocks. Anyway they sell breakfast crap at the concession stand before school, and they have a lot of cereal. I didn't see Smorz, but I asked about it. Chad wanted to know why I didn't just eat Cap'n Crunch. I told him that Cap'n Crunch was a pansy, and that even king vitamin could kick Cap'n Crunch's ass. And Smorz was cool because it has marbits that'll fit right up your nose. Dude, next time I score a box of Smorz, I swear I'm bringing my brother in to school to show these guys how he shoots marbits out his nose. If I know these losers they'd buy Smorz just to shoot em out of their own noses. anyway, my point is that Smorz needs a mascot. Like tony the tiger and crap. It would be a lot easier to talk up Smorz if I could just say "the Smorz guy can kick Cap'n Crunch right in his pansy purple crunchberries."

Staffer: Iesa McGettigan, Account Director
BzzCampaign: Ralph Cool
Reason for Choosing: When good flirting turns bad. This report is one of those awful, cringeworthy scenes that you see in a John Hughes movie. Oh, the lengths our agents will go to Bzz.

BzzAgent mommy2be Reports:
This was incredible beyond belief. We were in a line waiting to pay our respects to President Reagan when someone asked me what I was wearing cause I smelt yummy. One hot guy asking me this was kinda weird but ya know I jumped that right quick. I told him it was from my friend Ralph and he asked if Ralph and I

were intimate. I told him Ralph has been all over me for a few weeks and he asked if he had a chance at making Ralph disappear. I told him I couldn't part with Ralph and maybe I'd consider sharing. What I didn't realize is the whole thing was being shown on a local TV station and is still being run as a blooper since the guy was on a microphone. I have had crowds walking up to me all day today asking about "Ralph" so I'm Bzzing more and more.

Staffer: Kelly Hulme, Rewards & Fulfillment
BzzCampaign: Ralph Blue
Reason for Choosing: I chose it because it's a concise example of a real conversation between real people—a conversation that the people who developed the product probably never envisioned (even though this one is way less out-there than some of the other reports we receive)! A husband and wife are talking in the normal course of their day about pros and cons of the product, comparing it to other everyday scents, and calling BS on marketing-speak. Plus it shows that not all Bzz is glowingly positive or begrudgingly negative. (Also, I had to get some props in for Nantucket—where the waters are more often seaweed-red than anything resembling tropical blue!)

BzzAgent jultemp Reports:
I just received the Bzz package for Ralph Lauren Blue so I put some on to smell. I put it on each wrist and could smell a difference between the two. One smelled fine but a little too heavy for me, one smelled kind of unpleasant. (Don't know what that says about my wrist, but I had been traveling all day.) Then I asked my husband to smell my wrists and tell me what he thought. The first thing he said was, "Smells like shampoo." He also couldn't tell much difference between the wrists; both smelled like sham-

poo to him. Smelling like shampoo wasn't a bad thing to him, but it wasn't too exciting for me, especially since it didn't seem to jive with the Bzz literature. I also told him the "blue" was supposed to be like Nantucket waters, and he said the water there wasn't blue. So, so much for marketing literature. Anyway, I'll still Bzz about it since it may suit someone else.

Staffer: Rob Fitzgerald, Communications Developer
BzzCampaign: Holiday Inn Express
Reason for Choosing: This was a labor of love—to include as many Duran Duran song titles in my reply to askmom143 as I could. Just the '80s stuff, though. Sometimes I feel it is my civic duty to do stuff like this.

BzzAgent askmom143 Reports:
I happen to be a huge Duran Duran fan. The original lineup is back together once again & starting their American tour. I am going to one of the concerts this Sunday in Jacksonville, FL. I also belong to a group of about 12 fans online, so I thought I would mention the hotel to them as well. This is what I wrote to them: Hiya Ladies! Me again. Looks like things are finally working out for me. Robb got the time off & the return came in time so we are headed over to Jxvlle for the show!!!!!!!!!!!!!!!!!! I am so excited. We decided to not do it all in one day though. Too much on me, so we are going to spend the night somewhere over there. I am going to try to find one of these new Holiday Inn Expresses. I have heard such wonderful things about them like the awesome breakfast bar they have & they have lots of wonderful stuff in the bathrooms. I still have my collection of little soaps from the last tour don't you Sara? lol that was so much fun! Anyway, just thought I would mention that hotel idea for the rest of you gals when you are going to the shows. Tell you all about the show &

hotel when I get back. Love Ya All! Thanks for all the positive vibes, I knew it all work out that I got to go! Durannies ROCK.

Staffer: Matt McGlinn, Research Director
BzzCampaign: Lee One True Fit Jeans
Reason for Choosing: I like this, first, because it's absurd but clearly honest. The second reason I like it is because you see what a true recommendation can do, and how it can spread. I think this campaign has had the best BzzReports because the product rocked.

BzzAgent mermeyer921 Reports:
First let me add a disclaimer The actions you are about to read about are not normal behavior for someone as dignified and self-controlled as myself. That being said, here's my story. My True Fit jeans arrived in the mail on Wednesday. When I first pulled them out of the box, I thought to myself "Oh great! Another pair of wide leg pants." Now as a girl who was bestowed with something we call the Barber Family Calf Curse, this was not a good thing. Reluctantly, I tried them on. Not bad I thought, realizing that the pair sent to me were wide because they were boot cut; so I tried them on with my new brown boots. Niiice, I thought, bending down. Now normally, although it doesn't sound very sanitary, I do not like to wash my jeans too often because they become tight and are uncomfortable the first three times you wear them. When you are looking to shake "ya tailfeathas" tight jeans can leave you hanging at the table on purse patrol. This is background, more explanation and imperative to the story I am about to tell.

Fast forward to Saturday night. I went to a local hangout (Last Flight Out) wearing my new jeans with some girlfriends of mine. The night was going OK, we were having a couple of drinks and hanging out when I was drug out on the dance floor among my people, i.e., other drunk women who gyrate on the dance floor while spilling their drinks. "Damn, girl, this is my song," one of them mentioned. I was taking it all in stride and really enjoying the new drink I had discovered, fondly called by the bartenders in flight suits, Jumping Without a Parachute or JWAP for short. A JWAP consists of gin, vodka, tequila, rum, bourbon, a little triple sec, and a splash of grenadine. That is the last thing I remember. I woke up the next day with a major headache and not a real good idea of how I made it home. A call to a friend put it all in perspective. Apparently, after a few more JWAPs, a trip to the facilities was in order. Women always go in groups, so my friends and I trooped off to the ladies room. I don't really remember what happened next but I am told by my sources that while I was in there, I was complimented on my jeans, women do that, we are always commenting on someone's hair, shirt, butt, whatever. Not bad right, sounds pretty good even, sure, until she wanted to try them on. So we headed off to the stalls where I passed her my jeans underneath the stall to try on, much to the dismay of the eleven hundred ladies waiting in line. I set off a catalyst apparently because it became a free-for-all. Everyone was trying on the other person's clothes. Luckily, I made it home with the clothes I came with. Am I proud of my behavior? Not really, but I am apparently proud of my new Lee One True Fit Jeans.

Staffer: Seth Wylie, Research Analyst
BzzCampaign: Eats, Shoots & Leaves
Reason for Choosing: As many BzzReports as we read and surveys we put up, it can sometimes seem hard to believe that we have any significant number of agents out there. The more our agent population grows, though, the greater the chance that Bzz-Agents are going to start running into each other and find that they share something with each other that they may have never

shared with anyone before. It could be a common devotion to a brand or product, great stories about their Bzz, recognition that they're actually part of something greater than themselves, or just a quick "Isn't this a great way to get free stuff?!" (or all of the above). Whatever it may be, I, at least, am certainly looking forward to the day when I say, "Hey, are you Bzzing me?"

BzzAgent noraellen75 Reports:

I just had the BEST BZZ ever!! I was watching our local morning news. (Fox 26 morning news.) I was reading the ticker at the bottom of the screen as I always do. There was a story there about Britney Spears getting married again. It read, ". . . Spears, 22, married her 26-year old husband, a dancer in a secret weekend ceremony." I saw this ticker go by four times and finally couldn't stand it anymore! A dancer in a secret weekend ceremony? How about "a dancer, in a secret weekend ceremony"? I called the TV station! After five minutes of being transferred, I spoke with a production intern by the name of Kimberly. (It was very noisy in the background. I wish I had caught her last name!) I said, "I have a problem with the Spears story in your ticker." "What's the problem, exactly?" she asked very nicely. "It reads like Britney's husband is a dancer in a secret weekend ceremony," I said. "Uhm . . . hold on please," she said and I heard pages flipping. "Have you ever, by chance heard of the book, *Eats, Shoots and Leaves?*" I asked, just to get it in there. "Are you Bzzing me?" she asked and laughed! I was floored! "You're a Bzz Agent?" I asked, astonished! "Yeah," she said, "and I should know better! I've got that book! Have you ever told the panda joke?" "A few times," I said. I was completely floored! I could hear her typing and lots of noise going on around her. "Thanks for calling. I'll get that taken care of, OK?" she said. "Thanks a lot and have a great day, Kimberly!" I said. It was an abrupt conversation, but as soon as I'd hung up, I wished I had asked her BzzAgent name! Duh! But in my defense, it was very early! lol! Well, it took about ten minutes, but the ticker was corrected!! It was so cool to talk to someone who not only took me seriously, but knew exactly who I was and what I was doing!!

BzzAgents rock!!

Acknowledgments

First and foremost, I'd like to thank the BzzAgents. From day one, you've truly amazed us, inspired us, and engaged us to build a better system and to help companies see their customers as something other than targets. We've learned everything from you and continue to do so.

I would have never had the confidence to write this book without the help of two people: Esmond Harmsworth, the finest literary agent I know, who urged me to make this book a reality, and Michael B. Wright, who taught me—many years ago—about how much fun writing with a partner could be.

None of this would have become reality if Jon O'Toole hadn't believed that this idea "just might work," and we both thank Matt Fletcher for being the most loyal of business partners and having the nerve to stick around when he could have been playing poker or lassoing cattle.

Kurt Overberg, I owe you more than you could ever know. Thank you for teaching me HTML, introducing me to my wife, and then building every piece of technology we could ever imagine (in that order).

I'd like to thank Gene Quinn for declaring that we had moxie, for saying no, and for always listening.

Seth Godin for teaching, believing, and telling it like it is.

Of course, none of this could have been a reality without the amazing staff at BzzAgent, especially the Com-Dev team. You are the heart of this system and are pioneers in a new world of communication. You should be proud.

Wow, this wouldn't have been possible without my wife, Beth, who makes me laugh harder than anyone I know. Thank you for letting me live out this dream eighteen hours a day.

A very special thank you goes out to Rick Pascocello from Penguin Group, who took a risk on a very different idea and believed even when it was hard to. It's been a pleasure working with Penguin Group over the past few years, and specifically the team at Portfolio—Adrian Zackheim, Will Weisser, Allison Sweet, and Megan Casey—who made this book a reality.

Thank you to my family: Mom, Dad, Brad, and all of the pets that share our hearts.

And finally, this book is as much a part of John Butman as it is a part of me. John, thank you for teaching me about how perfect collaborations can work, and for giving me new awe and respect for the art of writing. It's been a pleasure. May we get a chance to do it again someday.

Index